MW00932196

"I'd urge any parents of small children to read it. I've found it brilliant! It encourages parents to listen to their instincts and their children, to have empathy for their toddlers and most of all – see their children for the amazing beings they are!"
Hannah Powell – Childcare Professional

"To say I dug this book is putting it mildly. I feel like Sam and I are long lost mother twins. I want to be her new best friend. She writes informally. This is not a textbook. This is not a highly scientific, rather inaccessible manual for experts. Reading this is like having an intimate conversation with a like minded friend."
Amy Brown – Zen Parenting

"It's amazing! A really gentle approach to the transition between baby to toddlerhood, so refreshing to read something I really can relate to as a mum."
Bethany Reynolds – Baby Wearing Consultant

Trust Me I'm A Toddler

A guide to parenting gently
and peacefully
through the toddler stage

For V,
for showing me the way.

And for Jed,
for listening to my dreams
and supporting
me in all that I do.

Contents

Introduction

My story starts a long time ago. I was desperate to get a job working with children, specifically babies. I loved being around children and for as long as I could remember I had loved mothering other people's babies.

My grandfather recently told me a story of my own childhood. He had come to babysit me and my two younger brothers, the youngest still a baby at the time, while my parents went on a rare night out. We were all settled in bed, the baby in his cot, when he woke and began screaming the house down. My grandfather, being of the *"Children should be seen and not heard"* generation, tried to calm him down to no avail. It was at this time that I woke and tried to help, but was told to get back to bed and he would stop crying eventually. My grandfather then went back downstairs and turned the TV up, leaving my brother to cry it out.

He tells me, a short time later he realised the baby was silent and snuck back upstairs to check on him. There he found me, just eight years old, brother in my arms, gently rocking and singing, as he slept peacefully. My grandfather was a very strict man and I know I would have been frightened of his reaction after disobeying his instructions, but he tells me that he was not angry. He was grateful. His instinct was telling him that this baby needed something but he was lost as to what to do. To find me soothing him to sleep made him proud, and he tells me that he could already see I would be a natural mother.

The instinct to parent, to know what this baby needed was already embedded in me as as child. So when it came to my first job working in a nursery, I felt excited and privileged to be a part of this early stage of development, to be trusted with someone's precious baby. But I began to encounter some confusing ways of thinking. I was told not to pick the babies up too much, that they couldn't be trusted to make their own decisions on whether they were hungry, or in need of a sleep.

The clock was the boss, and if they were due a sleep, they were going to be rocked against their will, or left to cry until they got the message. Being young and impressionable, I tried to get my head around these new ideas. I was told that it was best for the child and I assumed that these professionals knew best.

So one day when a new parent was visiting the nursery, and a baby was screaming it out in the adjoining sleep-room turning my insides to stone with every cry, I encountered a strange reaction. My manager was clearly uncomfortable with this new parent hearing the baby cry and asked me to go and see to him. I explained, as per the usual routine for this baby, that he would only cry until he fell asleep. That was what I had been taught wasn't it? But she insisted I went to him, and I did. Later she came and spoke to me, asking me to make sure the babies didn't cry when we had new visitors. Hold on a minute, if this is so normal and good for the babies, why are we ashamed of it? I began to realise what a terrible mistake I had made in being led by "the professionals" and letting go of my own instincts.

I stopped leaving the babies to cry, despite the mocking of the other staff. Over the course of my time working in nurseries I encountered the same ideas over and over again. *"Leave them to cry,"* ... *"Don't let them win,"* ... *"They will have to learn,"* ... *"It's no good for them to get attached to one person,"* ... *"He has been too spoilt by being picked up too often."* It's been a battle to hear my own instincts over the din of disapproval and has often been difficult to provide consistency to these children when so many of the staff have shut down their own instincts.

When I conceived my son I did so much reading and research. I knew I wanted him to have the best start to life and I didn't believe that this baby I was bringing into the world was out to control and manipulate me.

I decided to trust him and not hold back in any way. I gave myself up to instinct and what I learned was that those instincts are right. He has proved himself to be trustworthy without having to earn it. He has proved himself to be social, to have a desire to join in and help, and as he has grown from a baby to a toddler, he has shown me the way.

He has taught me to listen to him, to myself and to question conventional parenting. I have learned to stand up for my choices and protect his rights. I have learned that ultimately, toddlers deserve to be trusted.

This book will take you through the common (and not so common) issues parents face when their crawling baby becomes a curious toddler and starts voicing their own ideas. One of the things I will discuss in this book is how to set boundaries fairly and ensure that your child knows that they are still just as loved. I will provide you with the tools to not only cope with each situation, but to build a stronger, closer relationship between you both, and a more loving and accepting family unit. You don't have to declare war on your child, each day does not have to be filled with nagging, tantrums and tears. Read on if you want solutions that are respectful to the whole family and if you are ready to make a change.

CHAPTER 1

Why are the twos so terrible anyway?

Toddlers in our culture have a hard time. Before they even reach their first birthday they have already been the subject of much discussion: *"Is she good?" ... "Just wait until those tantrums start!" ... "What a diva!"*

It is so expected of our little darlings to become little tyrants, that people would almost be disappointed if they didn't perform. Don't underestimate the effect this has on our babies. If we adults spent our lives with such a shining spotlight highlighting our every action, and categorising it into good and naughty, we too might start to feel the pressure and crack under the strain.

People are far too quick to write off the feelings of a toddler solely based on their age. Have we not all had a day when we didn't want to be sociable, where we have felt tired and snappy, where we didn't want to face the busy crowds of the supermarket? Would you get cast off as *"terrible twenty six, thirty four, fifty five..."* if you pushed your dinner away, couldn't be bothered to pick up your clothes and put them away, or didn't want to sleep at your usual time one night? I doubt it.

Imagine if you were laying in the bath, loving the feel of the warm water, totally relaxing, when your partner/friend/mother suddenly decided that you were clean and pulled you out. How would that make you feel? Annoyed? Tearful? The human baby is dependent on their parents for their survival. They cannot bath themselves, feed themselves, dress themselves, and they rely on us as their carers to do these things for them.

However as your baby becomes a toddler, they will start to have their own ideas and preferences. Of course you can not let him stay in the bath for hours on end, but it is important that you acknowledge their feelings and empathise with them. Young as they are, talking through your actions will help them to understand in the long term why some things must be done, and will also help them to understand that you are on their side.

Imagine your own parent develops dementia and their care becomes your responsibility. Would you drag them kicking and screaming from an activity without warning, without an explanation? Or would you take the time to talk to them about why you must move on?

What is so important to remember is that

our children are just beginning to experience some very strong emotions, and they don't yet have the skills to explain how they are feeling. Once they become more verbal they may be able to explain these feelings, but more often than not they will be so overcome with the intensity of these emotions, that they will still need support working through them.

Not only that but their developing brains are not yet able to process disappointment, interruption and big feelings in the same way our adult brains can. How often do you hear parents say *"She is being so unreasonable!"* in reference to their toddlers? But if we remember that their brain is not yet fully developed in the skills of reasoning, that it is actually perfectly acceptable for a toddler to be unreasonable, perhaps we will move towards seeing the situation from their point of view, enabling us to help them to work through these feelings.

In dreading the "terrible twos" you are in essence creating a self fulfilling prophecy for your child.

They may have one hard week and before they know it, they are labelled terrible and whether you realise it or not, your reactions will change. It can be very difficult for parents facing these situations day after day, hour after hour to treat each incident separately and have patience and perspective with their child. Parents are struggling with their own unmet needs and often on the verge of exhaustion themselves, it can feel as if you have no more to give.

You are not alone in feeling this way. The transition from babyhood to the toddler stage is hard on most parents, and after months of meeting the few needs of your baby (milk, warmth, toileting and human contact), the addition of wants and desires to your child's needs can leave parents confused about what to do. For parents who have been consistent in meeting their baby's every need, it comes as a shock to realise that they can not always stop their child from expressing some strong emotions in the form of tears. It is no longer always healthy to say yes to every demand, *"Oh but Mummy, I want to run across this motorway!"* and this is the time where boundaries will be set.

The toddler years are an exciting and wonderful time where you will really get to know
your child's personality, and have the great
privilege of seeing the world through their
young eyes. Let's not waste one minute of that.

CHAPTER 2

Enabling independence

Your little one is branching out into the world, growing in confidence and full of curiosity. Everything is new and exciting and the urge to explore is overwhelming.

It can be hard as parents to know how much freedom to allow our children, how and when to set boundaries. The key is to say yes more than you say no. A toddler should feel free to discover their world and this starts at home. If there are things which are precious or danger-ous, remove them. Many parents feel frus-trated that their child won't listen and won't learn boundaries.

One mother told me in exasperation:

"When L started to move around, he was con-stantly playing with the DVDs on the shelf. Each time he went over to them I firmly told him, "No" and moved him away. But the second I turned my back he was straight over there again, pulling them from the shelves! If I took him away again he would arch his back and scream, throw himself on the floor. It was exhausting!"

A child being constantly restricted in their home environment is going to feel angry and frustrated. They have a genuine need to touch, taste and discover the items in their world. By restricting certain things, you are in effect making them even more enticing, and as such the child will find them totally irresistible. Your child is not intentionally disobeying you, they simply can not resist.

Of course there are always going to be times when you have to say no. For example, when the child is in danger. As soon as your little explorer masters the art of walking, a carry, sling or buggy will suddenly become a far less desirable place to be. Your "big boy or girl" will want to walk like mum and dad do much of the time. It is important to give them the chance to practice and develop their new skill as often as possible. Enabling them the freedom to explore will help them to burn up all that pent up energy and reduce their feelings of frustration.

When my son started walking he was very keen to get down and stretch his legs whenever we went out. If we were not in a big hurry I acquiesced. He would hold my hand, for stability as much as anything, and walk along beside me. If he broke away my reaction varied depending on the setting. If we were at the park, I backed off and gave him the freedom to explore. He would always stay close and return to me when he was satisfied.

If we were walking along a main road I set firm boundaries. If he wanted to walk, he had to hold my hand at all times. The rules from the very start were, no walking in the road, no playing with glass or dog mess, and no entering into people's gardens. It was important to me that we respected people's property and for obvious reasons, the road was out of bounds. If he did not want to follow my lead I would explain to him that we do not walk in the road and give him the option of continuing to walk and hold my hand, or to be carried.

Although just one year old and not yet able to verbalise his response, he understood through my actions. If he turned back to the road I would pick him up, reinforcing the message, *"We do not walk in the road, it is dangerous."*

Did he nod and say *"OK Mama!"* No. There were tears, kicks and shouts. He was furious at his freedom being restricted and unable to grasp the concept of danger. Farther on up the road I would give him the option to walk hold-ing my hand again, and if he strayed from the path I would repeat the whole scenario.

It can be hard to hear your child screaming and feel them kicking out against you. But in certain situations all you can do is empathise with their feelings, *"I know you wanted to pick that up, but it is sharp, so Mama had to stop you."* For your child to quickly learn the boundaries you MUST be consistent. It is no good moving the goalposts one day, letting them step in and out of the road because the traffic is quiet, or run into people's gardens because you are too tired to stop them. It is not fair on them as they won't understand why you are stopping them the next time, when it was fine last time.

The best methods to enable your toddler to learn these important safety guidelines are to:

- Set boundaries that are important to you, but think about why you are making each rule. Is it really necessary?

- Recognise that your child has a need to explore.

- Be consistent and reliable in your responses.

- Explain why you can't let them do something and what the consequence is, e.g. *"I can't let you walk in the road as it is dangerous. If you don't want to walk on the path with me I will put you in the sling."* This leaves the ultimate decision of their freedom up to them.

CHAPTER 3

Moving away from control, towards guidance

So many of the conventional approaches to discipline revolve around one thing – control. Parents feel that it is their responsibility to their child and to society, to control the behaviour and actions of their child. They feel under pressure that their family interactions look a certain way, that their child stands still while they wait at the post office, that they don't fidget and play with their cutlery they go out to eat.

They worry that if they buck the trend and stop challenging these behaviours, people will look on them as a negligent parent. Most of the time, nagging and punishing have little effect, and in most cases, usually provoke more of a scene as the child fights (often loudly) to protect their autonomy and independence.

But still the parent feels that at least they can be seen to be trying to correct this behaviour, the onlookers will offer sympathetic smiles and winks, showing that they can see you have your work cut out for you. Some may even step in and assist you in dealing with this handful of a child. It becomes adults against child, putting the child in the place of the powerless victim and the adult in the place of dictator.

Parents complain, *"If he had only listened to me and done as he was told, it never would have become such a scene!"*

But this is precisely the problem. Nobody likes to be controlled and told what to do, and what not to do. They like it even less when they are controlled in their every action and movement. *"Stop playing with that, stand still, put it down, hold my hand, come over here – No not there, HERE!!"*

For many children their whole day is directed from the moment they wake up, to the moment they go to bed, and actually for many, they don't get their freedom of choice during the night either. They want to sleep with Mummy but are sent back to their own bed. They are hungry or thirsty or need comfort, but are told that they are too big for milk and cuddles at night now. They are shown where to sit, what to eat, how to play, who to hug, the list just goes on and on. It's simply exhausting.

Imagine if you woke up and someone immediately started telling you what you needed to do. What if you decided to ignore these instructions, as you had a better idea of how to start your day, but in making that choice for yourself you were punished.

Children have such potential to learn, watch, develop and grow. They have an insatiable appetite for the world and for discovery. If we enable them to be free in their environment, guiding and insisting only when absolutely necessary, they will soon discover for themselves which things to repeat and which things to file away under "a learning experience."

> If a child falls when climbing, they remember. They step more carefully next time.

If they are picked up and carried off before they get the experience of falling, then one day they might climb too fast, too high and get a bigger bump when you are not around to rescue them.

A controlled child will either rebel or grow into a controlled adult. And I mean that in the worst sense of the word. You will find yourself full of frustration at their lack of initiative, their willingness to be led astray by their peers who also like to tell them what to do. They will have had little opportunity to make their own decisions and figure out things for themselves.

They may find it difficult to entertain themselves or use their imagination, so used to having someone there telling them where they should put the puzzle piece, what colour they should be using to draw their cat.

But what about the child who has not been controlled? The child who draws a purple cat and chooses not to wear his shoes so he can feel the blades of grass between his toes. The child who has had bumps and bruises and learned quickly the safest route up onto the windowsill, the table top, the slide. He is able to make his own decisions about what he wants from life, and he knows he will be supported in going for it. He is able to use his imagination, to conjure up images of how an object might feel and taste, because he has already had the freedom to explore so many things along his path. And what about the adult he grows into? An adult with determination, courage, independence, creativity, initiative and self assurance.

Isn't that the adult we hope our child becomes?

Control is so ingrained in conventional parenting, but it doesn't have to be. Our children are trustworthy, but for some reason, we feel they have to earn that trust. It is rare, however that they even get far enough to prove that their intentions were good. And controlling is a very easy habit to fall in to. You start when your baby begins crawling (if not before) moving them away, redirecting them, taking things away from them, and before you know it, their every move is up for criticism. A better way would be to start as you mean to go on. Make everything safe within reason, don't leave your laptop open next to a pint of water, move anything you really don't want them to get hold of and put it away, out of sight.

Create a "yes" environment that is exciting and stimulating to explore and discover, where they can feel free and unrestricted. Let them experience all that this world has to offer.

CHAPTER 4

Separation anxiety and returning to the work place

Once your baby reaches the age where they notice you leaving the room, they may begin to experience separation anxiety. This is likely to carry on well into the toddler years, especially with new people or in new situations. One of the benefits to attachment parenting is that in providing a strong grounding for your child from the start, they will one day feel confident and be happy to branch out independently.

Toddlers who have not had this grounding early on, may appear more outgoing and confident on the surface, than an "AP" child, but in the long term, the child who has been able to break away from the security of their mother at their own pace, will be the one who reaps the benefits.

During the toddler years, children may find it very difficult to be away from their primary caregiver. This can become as extreme as not wanting to be left with family members, even if they have been happy to be left with them in the past. This is a common time for parents to complain that their once independent and happy child is now clingy and shy, and many begin to worry that they should be breaking them of these habits and teaching them how to branch out into the world.

However, rushing a child towards inde-pendence before they are ready is not only un-necessary, but is likely to raise other issues within the child. They may regress with certain skills or behaviours, or may start to act out in other ways. This time can be especially hard for parents to cope with, as many will be fin-ishing maternity leave to begin a return to work, coinciding with this sensitive period.

For parents who are still making decisions about the return to work, if you have the op-tion to delay it, or explore other avenues such as working from home, this might be worth considering. There are many companies that facilitate working from home and it is worth discussing your options with your employer. Maternity leave is also a great time to explore your own interests and goals, as you find your-self with more time to think. It might be the right time for you to do some research on start-ing your own passion based business.

If you choose to do this you may be able to work while your toddler naps and in the even-ings or early mornings. However, if you feel you need more time to get your work done, a

Nanny who comes to your home may be a good option, as your child is able to stay in familiar surroundings and you are able to periodically take breaks to reconnect with them.

Working at home is not always a possibility for everyone though, and as a childcare professional of many years, I want to give you my experience and personal tips for choosing the right fit for your family. I should point out that I have experience running a baby room at a busy nursery, working with children with widely ranging disabilities whilst running children's after school clubs, and am now working part time as a Childminder from home. Although I have some bias, I hope to present the different options available to you honestly, to enable you to make up your own mind.

One option which may work out to be the most affordable, is to make an arrangement for a relative to provide childcare while you work. If you have a willing family member, this can be a wonderful solution, as your child will benefit from spending time and forming a stronger attachment to someone in their extended family.

The biggest plus for choosing a family member is that you know that they are always going to be a part of the child's life, which is not necessarily the case with the other options. You will also know the person well and be able to decide if you are comfortable with their style of childcare.

It is important to establish ground rules from the very beginning of these arrangements though. Before you make any decisions you should sit down together and discuss your expectations. It is important to cover your wishes on discipline, what you would hope for your child during your time away from them, and how the relative would deal with certain scenarios. Check with them how many hours they are comfortable to provide childcare and whether it will be in your home or theirs.

Often relatives can over commit themselves when it comes to helping out, and may not admit to struggling. Make sure that you don't take advantage and that you periodically check to see how the arrangement is working out for all parties. I would recommend starting on a trial period so that you can see how it is working out, and make changes where necessary. If the relative is enjoying the time with your child, but struggling with the hours you require, split childcare is a good option. You could split the hours between a few relatives or with a Nanny, Childminder or nursery.

Option One – Nanny

A Nanny is someone who comes to your own home to care for your child. It can be expensive if you only have one child, but the hourly rate tends to be the same for one as it is for multiple children, so it could work out as a very affordable option if you have several children. Nannies are not all regulated in the same way, and in the UK there is no requirement for them to be trained or police checked. You can find a Nanny through either independent advertising or by going through an agency.

This will come with a cost, but the agency will vet the applicants to find a good match for your family. The advantages of a Nanny are that the child is able to stay in their familiar surroundings, the Nanny will become a part of your family and enable your child to form a secure attachment, and you are able to set the standards about your expectations for childcare and activities. A Nanny is also a common choice for children with disabilities or additional needs. They are able to give one to one attention and some will specialise or have experience in particular areas.

The disadvantages of a Nanny are that they could leave at any time, you will have to do paperwork as you are their employer, such as tax returns and CRB checks, and you may want to pay for them to attend courses on first aid, play or on additional needs.

Option Two – Childminder

Childminders (home daycare) have many benefits too. It is worth visiting several to get a feel for how each setting works as each Childminder can vary hugely in the way they run their setting. Childminders can often take on too many children, and I would be looking for someone who has a good balance and can meet my child's needs, without the fear of him getting lost in the crowd. One advantage of a Childminder, as with a Nanny, is the ability for your child to form secure, long term attachments to their care giver. Often parents worry that they don't want their child to become too attached to someone else, in the fear that it will take away from their own relationship with their child. This however, is not the case.

It is healthy and natural for a child to form strong attachments.

It is much better that they do this than switch off and shut down. For children who are adopted in their toddler years, it is the ones who have learned to attach to a foster carer who are then more able to transfer that attachment on to their adoptive parents.

Those children who spent their early years languishing in orphanages, are far more likely to struggle with forming attachments and letting anyone else try to meet their needs. Your child will feel far more confident and secure in childcare if they are able to attach to a trustworthy adult. It will compliment your relationship, rather than compete with it.

Childminders are able to provide a relaxed home from home environment and many will do activities similar to those you might do with them. Baking, painting, trips to a park, farm or aquarium, children's groups, access to the outside and good quality resources. On the other end of the scale are Childminders who stick the TV on and walk away, ignore the children or discipline harshly. Ask to see photographs of the things they get up to and for references from other parents.

Childminders are different from Nannies in that they make the rules and plan their days. It is important to ask them about what a typical day looks like, the type of activities your child will have access to, and their philosophy on childcare. Again this will vary hugely between Childminders, and it may take some searching to find the right match.

Childminders and Nannies are both a risk of being unreliable. If they are unwell, on holiday, or suddenly give you notice, you may have to come up with an alternative arrangement. It is a good idea to have a back up plan in place for unforeseen circumstances.

Option Three – Nursery

That leads me to the final option I want to discuss, nursery (daycare). Nurseries are going to be your best option in terms of reliability, as it is very rare that they close for sickness and they are often able to call in agency staff in an emergency. They will usually have more resources and activities on hand for your child to try, but be aware that more toys is not always better.

Nurseries are less likely to take daily trips out into the community, but should have access to a garden. Ask how often your child will be able to play outdoors and if they have the freedom to go outside when they please. If this is the first time your child is going into nursery, you may find their nap becomes disrupted as there will be much more going on around them. Even if there is a dedicated sleep room, there will be strange new noises and smells, keeping them more alert than usual.

The biggest disadvantage to a nursery is the high turnover of staff. Generally your child will be assigned a key worker who has the responsibility of recording their development and milestones. The parent doesn't tend to get a say in which Nursery Nurse becomes the key worker and may not get much chance to get to know them.

Even if the toddler does form an attachment to some of the staff, this will be disrupted as they get older. Nurseries are split into rooms based on age, and children tend to move up when they reach two, and then again at three. This means getting to know a whole new group of staff and a whole new environment. There may be other children who move up with them and provide some familiarity, but although their key worker may stay with them to settle them in for a short while, there will be no trusted adult who stays with them through their whole journey.

The number one piece of advice I can give you when choosing the right childcare for your family is to follow your instincts. Watch how your child behaves in each environment and take their lead in showing you what they need.

If your child is experiencing separation anxiety and finding new situations uncomfortable, whatever option you choose, I would encourage you to make it a very slow transition. Book as many visits as possible for you to go with him to the new setting. Stay with him for as long as he needs. Make staff aware that you are staggering your visits and do not intend to leave your child alone yet. Allow him to join in and explore at his own pace, so as not to push him into an uncomfortable situation.

As an ex nursery worker, I know that parents are often encouraged to leave without saying goodbye so as not to upset the child, usually as he begins to play. Although the staff have good intentions, you know your child best.

> Don't be pushed into anything you are uncomfortable with.

If your child has just built up the confidence to go off and explore, it will be quite a shock for him to later discover that he can't find you and he can't recognise anyone.

By drawing out your visits, you may seem an oddity to the staff, but you will be able to reassure your child that they are somewhere safe. You will be able to see how he reacts to his key worker and how she reacts to his needs. You will be able to see if he is happy in this environment and if the pace suits him. When you feel that he has someone he can call on if he is frightened, hurt or just in need of someone, and feeling more at home in his surroundings, this is the time to back away.

It is much better to say goodbye and explain that you will be back soon. For the first time, don't go away for more than an hour, so he can trust that you have kept your promise, that you will always come back for him. Over the course of visits, slowly lengthen this time, always taking his needs into consideration, staying longer with him if he needs you. In my experience, the children who have had this gradual and gentle start to childcare are much happier than those left suddenly. For those "abandoned" children, their first few sessions are usually spent sobbing in their new caregivers arms, who gentle as they might be, is a stranger to this child.

After this period of huge distress the child will usually withdraw into themselves, often becoming very upset on the journey into child-

care and, if the childcare in question is a nursery, struggling immensely if the key worker is
not around. It may seem over the top, but your
child's well-being and security is worth it, so
make your plans early and give them the time
they need.

CHAPTER 5

Mine, yours and ours – Toddlers CAN share

In the world of a toddler, sharing is not always easy. Once they get hold of that much desired object, they don't always feel like giving it up. Snatching and hoarding can become common behaviours and everyone assumes that this is the norm. But toddlers are fully capable of sharing, in the right situations.

The way to approach sharing is to understand that your toddler has certain limitations in their patience and willingness. They may be quite happy to share the first time, then the second, but they might suddenly stop sharing when they reach their level of comfort. This is an opportunity for you as their parent to show your child that you are on their side, and that you understand that they have a strong need to hold on to this particular item.

Often parents step in far too soon to break up a situation between children. In doing this the children don't get the opportunity to work through the disagreement by themselves. If you give them time, you may find that it resolves itself, although often not in the way we would have resolved it.

For a parent, it can be heart wrenching to see someone else's child come over and take something from your own child. You want to jump immediately to their defence and get it back for them. But before you act hastily, step back and observe the scene. Is your child actually bothered? Or have they moved on to something else? Perhaps they have even decided that the other child should not have taken their toy and gone to get it back for themselves. Although these situations between toddlers make us feel uncomfortable, could it be that we are not always needed to referee?

Your child may take the toy back out of the child's hands and the child may accept it, or they may try to reclaim it once again. If it becomes a scuffle, here is a good point to step in and defuse the situation, but try to wait for one of the children to indicate to you that they need a bit of backup. There is a big difference between bullying and standing up for yourself. Children can learn a lot from each other without the involvement of adults. By staying in tune with what is going on, ready to step in if you are needed, you can give children the time to work out a solution.

If you are finding that it is your own child who is struggling with sharing, there is a lot you can do.

Sharing is a learned behaviour, and the best way for your child to learn to share is through role modelling sharing and generosity yourself. If your household is a world of *"mine"* and *"yours"* your child will quickly learn to protect *"their things."* Toddlers are told over and over again, *"This is Mummy's, this one is yours,"* as they are moved away from something or refused something.

They are told they can't eat this because it's yours, can't have that because it's mine. The idea of ownership is pushed from our own beliefs onto our children as soon as they start crawling. Let me ask you, if you are not prepared to share *"your things"* with your child, how on earth are they going to learn the art of sharing?

The *"mine"* phase is difficult to avoid completely as your child will likely be exposed to other children going through the same struggles, which may put the idea of holding on to their things into their heads. But if they have a good grounding of sharing and come from a family where there is no *"mine and yours,"* where they are free to have a spoonful of the cereal you are eating, where they can borrow the pen you are using in exchange for this pencil they have found, where they can sip water from the same glass as daddy, then the idea of sharing becomes not something to fear, but something that comes completely naturally to them.

The common scenario when toddlers are fighting over something is that the parent steps in and talks about taking turns, simultaneously gently (but forcibly) taking said item from one child to give it to the other. I want to offer a different option.

If your child has something that another child desperately wants, talk to them about it. When myself and my son find ourselves in such a situation, I say, *It seems that he has a strong need for this particular toy, do you think you could give it to him and play with this one instead?* Here I would offer a similar toy to my child. I typically ask this only of my own child, as many of the children we encounter don't have the same family background to sharing. However, when your child belongs to a sharing family, giving up this particular toy is not the end of the world to them. Here they have the chance to investigate a new exciting toy, and he can see that this other child has a strong need to have the first toy.

It is very rare that my child would refuse to give his toy up. However, if he is overtired, unwell or irritable for some other reason, he is much less willing. I need to respect his choices as an individual. If he refuses to give up a particular toy, that is his choice to make. It may mean comforting and finding a distraction for the other child, but if I were to snatch the toy from my sons hands and give it away before his very eyes, I would be reinforcing so many behaviours and ideas in both of the children; *Adults can snatch so it's OK for me to do it too. If I want something, I take it. What I say doesn't really matter, as it's only going to be overruled if an adult doesn't agree.*

These are not lessons that I want to teach children. Taking the toy from them may solve the issue in the short term, but in the long run it is far more likely to create hoarding tendencies and bigger disagreements.

In parenting, we should always have one eye on the future. How is this action going to affect his long term behaviour, his feelings of trust in me? Quick fixes are generally not the answer. Changing behaviours means changing your whole outlook and adjusting your attitudes. Look inwards and see how generous you are being with your family. Let go of your own hoarding tendencies, it's all so much more fun when we relinquish ownership and break bread together.

I have encountered some situations where my son has found himself in regular tussles with another child, resulting in each of them taking what the other has over and over again, creating anguish and upset to all parties. When this occurs, I think it is important to focus on the deeper needs. If the situation is becoming fraught, it tends to be the children's underlying feelings coming out, projecting themselves onto this particular item. When this happens, I try to remove my son from the situation, rather than focus on removing the item.

I gently explain that we need to calm down and take him somewhere to have a cuddle and reconnect. He might nurse or I might be able to see that he is hot and tired, hungry or unwell. Whatever I identify as the deeper need, I do my best to meet it. On occasion that will mean leaving a social gathering, a group, a friends house, as I can see that my son is not able to cope with it in his current state. It's OK to put their needs first and leave when you can see the situation is taking a downward spiral. Becoming repeatedly worked up over sharing is often the first sign that there is something else going on. Let your child know that you are there for them, whatever the situation, by taking the time to see what is really going on.

Learning to take turns is a valuable lesson but takes time and clear instructions.

- Reinforce and repeat your message gently whilst accepting their stage of development and their capabilities. If they are not yet ready for this concept, let it go and try again a month or two later.

- When a child learns the art of taking turns, and accepts the concept, it is a good idea to offer them a distraction or another activity to fill their time while they are learning to wait, *"We will read a story and then it will be your turn on the rocking horse!"* Stick to any promises you make though!

- Having too many toys can actually create more difficulties between children. Try to minimise your toys at home opting for more open ended resources. Children like to copy each other, so instead of having one expensive toy to fight over, several of the same things such as containers, spoons or boxes will give less opportunity for conflict and more time for playing and learning together.

CHAPTER 6

Brushing teeth

Ah, it sounds so simple. *"Don't forget to brush her teeth!"* your partner calls as you take your little one up for the night. To some parents this sentence fills them with dread, knowing that the next twenty minutes are going to be fraught with tears, resistance and a battle that leaves you both feeling defeated.

Bear in mind that I am not a dentist and can not give you first hand accounts of what happens when you do not brush your baby's teeth. However I have done some research on the subject, and my overall findings are that dental hygiene is very important, and that unhealthy baby teeth can cause problems for your child in the future.

The biggest issues with not brushing your child's baby teeth, are that it leaves them susceptible to cavities. This is especially true if they are eating processed and sugary foods. These cavities can form deep holes in the baby tooth and become infected. If it goes deep enough to reach the adult tooth just beneath the surface, it can affect it, causing a brown or black spot that will be permanently visible on the adult tooth.

Of course cavities and mouth infections are

also quite painful for the child, and the need to have early dental work can create life long fears in some children.

If it becomes necessary to have a baby tooth removed, the hole will usually fill in, making it more difficult for the adult tooth to later emerge, and possibly causing the tooth to come up at a crooked angle. The tooth may come up in the wrong place as it does not have the baby tooth to guide its path. This can cause overcrowding of the teeth which may lead to more difficulty in keeping them clean and will prompt many children to have braces in their future.

This knowledge can put a pressure on parents to keep those little teeth clean. But your toddler senses your determination and a power struggle ensues, making that twice daily tooth brushing, a stressful and upsetting event.

There are a lot of things you can do to make tooth brushing a calm, and even enjoyable event.

One of my favourite pieces of advice to give to parents is to let your child or someone else brush your teeth. How does it feel to have someone poking a foreign object into your mouth? Unpleasant? Unsettling? Doing this will enable you to empathise with your child and understand one of the reasons they resist you doing the same to them.

Here are some of my favourite tips for keeping those little pegs clean and sparkly:

- Do it at the start of your bedtime routine when tiredness has not yet taken over leaving little patience for being interfered with.

- Brush your own teeth at the same time. Children love to imitate adults and this is a great way of encouraging your toddler to brush their teeth.

- Hold your hand over their hand to ensure that the teeth are getting a thorough brushing without taking away your child's involvement.

- Turn the tap on and let them dip their brush in the water and chew on the brush. It may become a game that lasts a while but the teeth are getting cleaner and tooth brushing becomes a fun task, rather than a time of stress.

- Get creative in inventing new hilarious games. A laughing child has an open mouth and you can make a fun experience of this routine.

- Let them use a soft adult toothbrush like Mummy's or Daddy's to do the job.

- Pretend to brush your own teeth with their brush and alternate brushing your teeth with brushing their teeth.

- Distract them with the light switch. While they are turning it on and off, their mouth will open and you can get a few brushes in before it closes. Repeat, repeat, repeat!

- Brush their teeth while they are in the bath, busy investigating the water.

- Try another room of the house if they

are too focused on avoiding the tooth-brush in the bathroom.

• Make a routine of you brushing their teeth first and then handing over the job to them, so they feel involved.

• Try not to rush them. If they are really in to brushing their teeth one day, let them explore that. Rushing them is likely to take all the fun out of the activity.

• Always talk through what you are do-ing so they know what is happening and how much longer it's going to take. *"Nearly done, just the back ones to clean now."* Be honest so they can trust you. It's a good idea to do them in a familiar order, front, top, bottom and back, so they can keep track and learn the se-quence.

• Even if you never get the toothbrush past their lips, try to keep the routine going for twice daily teeth brushing, going into the bathroom, putting the paste on the brush and spending a few minutes "brushing our teeth." They may not actually get brushed, but try not to get too stressed about it, keep it fun and as your child gets older it will get easier.

- If all else fails, give your toddler their toothbrush to suck and chew on at regular intervals throughout the day (without toothpaste). This gives them the independence they crave and chewing on a toothbrush will be beneficial for their teeth.

Keep in mind that to reduce the chances of cavities, sugary drinks and food should be avoided where possible, and toddlers should have water and/or breast milk to make up the majority of their drinks. Be aware of the hidden sugars in foods and check the ingredients list if you are buying something pre-prepared. These early years are the best time to form ingrained habits in dental hygiene and healthy eating.

CHAPTER 7

Bedtime and Naps

You know your own child better than anyone else, and you also know if they are the type of child who will fall asleep at the drop of a hat, or if they need a precise and predictable routine. For most children, they fall somewhere in between, coping better with predictability, but without the stress of clock watching and inflexibility thrown into the mix. Bedtime is one of those situations that could easily become stressful under the right (or wrong) circumstances.

The activities of the day have worn you all out, and you know that you will have some time to yourself once your little one is sleeping soundly. This can make some parents rush bedtime in an urge to get their down time, but doing so often backfires, making bedtime a stressful and lengthy event.

You can't force a child to sleep and there is no point in trying. If you get stressed, your child will sense this and find it even harder to settle down. So the most important attribute we can bring to the bedtime routine, is a mellow attitude. Take a deep breath, accept that it will take exactly the amount of time that is required and that no amount of hurrying, stress or anger is going to make it go any quicker.

Pinpoint which part of the bedtime routine is not working and then you can begin to remedy it.

For my spirited son, the times when he would become the most upset (which at first seemed completely unreasonable to me) were when he was tired and I would try to take him from one room to the next. We would finish our story and I would say, *"OK, let's go to bed,"* and as soon as I lifted him off the floor he would scream and squirm. The same happened when I would place him down on the bed, he would go crazy and take a long time to calm down.

I tried a number of techniques, singing a familiar song each time, giving him a five minute warning but it wasn't the going to bed that was the issue, it was the control. One day I put bed time in his hands. He chose his story as usual and then when we finished reading I stood up and said, *"Let's put the book back and go to bed."* He passed me the book and watched me put it on the shelf. Then I held out my hand and we walked to the bedroom together. When we got there I got myself settled on the bed and left him at the side. He walked around one side, then back and held up his arms to be picked up. I picked him up, fed him and he was out cold in five minutes flat. No tears before bedtime! Such a simple change of me giving the control back to him made a world of difference.

Toddlers need to be involved in decisions that involve them. Take their preferences into consideration and give them options that you can both be happy with. Having a set routine in place that instead of focusing on the clock, focuses on the sequence of events that precedes bedtime, will help to eliminate any confusion or resistance.

If you always for example: brush teeth, get undressed, read a story, turn the lights off and nurse to sleep, it enables your child to know what's coming next, so they don't feel so out of control and like a passenger rather than a participant.

There is no point putting your child to bed when they are wide awake. You may feel that you *need* them to go to bed as you have had a particularly tiring day. You may feel that you don't have time to wait for your child to wind down. But in waiting until they are tired, bedtime will be much quicker and smoother than if you try to get them to sleep when they are not yet ready. Wait for the signs of tiredness to show. Irritability, rubbing their eyes and yawning, or requesting to nurse more frequently are signs that you should be heading off to get ready for bed.

By keeping track of your child's tired signs you can begin to form a routine and know when to expect them. Then if you like, you can begin taking them up to bed at around the same time each night, of course taking into consideration variations in nap times and how busy and active a day they have had.

Above all, relax into the moment. We spend so long looking forward to an evening of peace and quiet, that so often we miss out on what is one of the most special and loving times of the day. Try to be fully present with your child throughout this process, and instead of thinking about what still needs to be done, just enjoy what you are doing right now. Bedtime allows us the chance to reconnect after the day. To talk to each other as you help to get them dressed, to cuddle up and read a story, lingering over the pictures and seeing what you can spot.

Laying in the dark with your toddler clambering over you could be seen as a stressful affair, but see it from their point of view instead. They have you all to themselves and are enjoying every minute as they become more and more tired.

When my son was first born I read over and over the same advice given by many people. The advice was to never make full eye contact with my baby or to talk to him at night time, for fear that I would over-stimulate him and he would be eternally awake. I have to say that this advice feels completely unnatural to me. When he was younger he would climb on me, peer into my eyes and do all manner of amusing things before he went to sleep. I would smile at him, make eye contact, whisper to him, and we would usually have a few fits of giggles before he nodded off.

Now that he is understanding the world more, he likes to recap his day as he is drifting off to sleep. He tells me what he has seen and I love to hear his point of view and which activities stuck in his mind. Maybe it takes a few more minutes for him to fall asleep than if I were to ignore him. But do you know what? He falls asleep with a smile on his face, having just had some great fun with a parent who he knows loves him completely.

The toddler stage is often a time of disruption to the family's sleeping arrangements. Many children will have been co-sleeping or bed sharing up until now, and others will already be in their own room. During this phase a child in their own room may suddenly decide that they no longer want to go to bed alone. This can be a trigger for some children to begin fighting against bedtime, creating games and excuses for staying up. They may begin waking more at night and asking to come in bed with you, or perhaps you are already bringing them in due to sheer exhaustion.

Society dictates that if you haven't already, now is the time to put your foot down and enforce a separation, moving your toddler into a room of their own. But how important is this really? The novelty of children having their own room is reserved only for the children of rich developed countries with money and space to provide several bedrooms in the family home. Children in poorer places can be found sleeping in a family bed or floor mat, along with their parents and siblings for many, many years.

People will tell you that sharing your bed with your child is not only damaging and restrictive to your romantic relationship (if you are in one), but also preventing your child from branching out, becoming independent and learning to sleep alone. They will tell you that these things are vital to their development, and may accuse you of being unwilling to let go. The reality is that these are simply unfortunate myths and opinions.

A child who is welcome in his parents bed is actually likely to be far more independent, secure and confident than a child who sleeps alone. He is more likely to have greater self esteem and fewer fears associated with bedtime. Bed sharing also enables a closeness and connection between the whole family that is missed when we sleep apart. It provides the feeling of being united and a team, which will make daytime parenting easier. A connected, happy and secure child who knows they will be responded to day AND NIGHT is much more likely to respect your wishes and join in with the family rituals.

The fear that your relationship will suffer and your child will never learn to sleep on their own is unfounded. In much the same way that a child will naturally wean from the breast if the decision is left in their hands, (See Breastfeeding through the toddler stage) a child will one day reach a point where they are keen to move out of the family bed and into their own room. Ask around and you will be lucky to find any fifteen year olds still regularly sleeping with mum!

The difficulty here is not the co-sleeping in itself (many parents mourn the end of this special time), but in adjusting our attitudes and perspective. As humans it is our evolutionary expectation to sleep surrounded by others. In the days when we were all living in hunter gatherer tribes, a child left to sleep alone would be gobbled up in no time at all by a hungry predator.

These days, our homes may be built with brick, safe and warm, but that doesn't change the fact that our instincts are still programmed to feel this way. To a child who has not yet learned to ignore his evolutionary instincts, sleeping alone just feels wrong.

> Bringing your child into your bed, is simply parenting as nature intended.

It is quite the opposite of spoiling, indulging or damaging them. So if co sleeping is an option for you, why not give it a try? After the novelty wears off and the new routine is established, you may find that you all sleep more soundly.

Not all families find bed sharing possible, and sometimes children become ready for their own bed during the toddler stage. If this is the case, it is important to remember that their night time needs will still remain.

Even with a child in their own room, it is important to be flexible and tackle bedtime in a gentle and responsive manner. This will help to reduce their fears and resistance to bedtime. Remembering that their fears are genuine evolutionary impulses, rather than a method to manipulate or mess you around, will enable you to fully empathise with them and come up with creative solutions to chase the monsters away, and invite in the good dreams.

Naps can become hit and miss once the toddler years arrive, but the majority of toddlers really do need that block of time to unwind during the day. When there is too much going on, it can be easy for naps to be missed and difficult for your toddler to get the rest they need. When a toddler is regularly skipping their usual nap, it can be easy for parents to take advantage of this extra time and fill it up with more activities and errands, but this can easily lead to an over tired and uncooperative child. Even if they don't use the time to sleep, they will still benefit from a dedicated quiet time, looking at books or doing some relaxed free play at home.

Work out the time of day when your little one is most sleepy, before they become over tired, then aim to make this a time for relaxing and unwinding, preferably in a familiar homely environment, and not planning anything too stimulating or exciting for this period. Missed naps are often to blame for a whole host of issues from tantrums to irritability, and you will both have an easier time of it if you are not sleep deprived.

Nap time may seem like a perfect time for you to do the housework, but I urge you to use nap times to rest yourself, and do something fulfilling for you. Not only will you benefit from giving back to yourself, but refuelling your own energy levels will help you to parent with patience and understanding during the rest of the day. On top of those reasons, if you need more, your toddler will get so much out of watching you do the household jobs, learning and advancing in his development as he imitates your actions and gets involved in the household tasks!

CHAPTER 8

Biting

Biting is a common phase amongst toddlers and can be triggered by a number of causes. Tiredness, hunger, feeling uncomfortable and threatened in a situation and teething are just a few. It could also be a cry for more attention if they are feeling like they haven't had enough time with you. Toddlers are not malicious but they have not got the ability to reason with themselves, and stop themselves from giving in to the urge to bite.

I have heard all sorts of methods that parents use in order to get their child to stop biting. One worryingly common idea is that the parent should bite the child back in order to curb this habit immediately. But what does this really teach a child? Children want to please their parents and they want to be just like them. If you bite your child back it shows them that it's okay for adults to bite, which could easily result in imitation.

It also hurts them, humiliates them, and damages the relationship between parent and child. They will feel angry, scared and helpless and this is not a good recipe for positive behaviour and strengthening the parent child connection.

Biting can be used in frustration against playmates, siblings or other adults. To discourage biting and prevent it from becoming a habit, there are a few things you can do. The first is to make sure that your toddler has had enough sleep, and enough to eat and drink throughout the day. Take snacks along with you to offer if she seems agitated and postpone your plans until nap or quiet time is finished.

Hunger and tiredness are responsible for a whole host of behavioural issues, and will cause your toddler to have a short fuse and react more strongly to situations that would otherwise not phase her.

If you know that your child always "targets" certain children with her biting, discreetly observe her whilst she is playing near the other child, and be ready to intercept with a distraction when she goes to bite. I always encourage parents to expect the best from their child and give them the benefit of the doubt, but if you place yourself in a position where you could easily intervene without looking like you are hovering waiting for her to bite, you can prevent another child getting hurt, and offer alternative solutions to your own toddler, talking about her feelings so she can learn how to describe her frustrations.

Being aware of your child and their changing moods will enable you to see if there was a particular event that triggered the attempt to bite, enabling you to work through this in partnership with your child.

Children who do not yet have the language skills to describe how they are feeling and what they need, are more likely to react physically to a frustrating situation, be it through biting, tantrums, snatching, or something else. All children learn to speak at different rates and the majority of children will learn to talk, so it is important not to compare your child's abilities to those of others, or worry unnecessarily. Trust your instincts on this and seek advice if you feel your child needs additional support.

One thing you can do to help your child develop their language skills, is to talk her through each situation and guess at how she might be feeling, supplying the words she needs to be able to tell you.

"You are feeling sad and angry because you were playing with the ball and another child took it away."

"You are feeling too hot and need a rest in the shade."

"I am feeling hungry and need a break, do you too?"

"It looked like you were really having fun on the beach!"

Try to get into the habit of doing this, and also make sure you are making full eye contact with your child each time you speak to her. Spend time reading books together and talk about them as you do, guessing at the feelings of the characters and choosing stories with gentle and caring story lines.

If you should miss a bite, what should you do? As her parent you can go over to the children and console the bitten child with a big hug, if they are open to it, or alternatively make the child's parents aware that they need comforting. You can talk to your toddler and explain that he is crying because that bite hurt him.

> It is important to make it clear that you are sad about the bite, but not angry with your child, only confused at this behaviour.

Whilst you are comforting the bitten child, your own child may approach in curiosity, she may laugh and run off, or she may herself cry at the situation. This is a good opportunity for your child to begin to learn to empathise with the pain of others.

If your child wants a hug too, don't hold back. She may be just as upset by the whole incident and need reassurance from you. If you feel that it was done for attention, you can remedy that by ensuring you spend more one on one time with your child, so they never feel like they have to resort to biting to get it.

As the other child moves away, try to keep your child with you for a hug or to nurse. Spend a bit of quiet time together, resetting the mood and letting them know that they are still loved. Focus your attention on uncovering what their need may be in this situation. It could be time to say your goodbyes to everyone and head off in order to meet those needs.

Sometimes the bite is directed at an adult rather than another child. This can be easier to deal with as you can focus your full attention on helping your child to work through this, rather than splitting it between the two.

Often when a child bites an adult it is down to over excitement and over stimulation. It could be a game that got out of hand, a method of dispelling pent up energy, or a way of getting your attention back when you have lost focus on the activity. It could also be a display of frustration if another baby has joined the family and your attentions are split between your two children.

If a child bites you or another adult, ensure you make it clear immediately that it caused you pain and is not acceptable behaviour. A simple *"Ouch, that hurt, don't bite Mummy again, it makes me sad,"* is usually enough. Again, focus on what need remains unmet and try to remedy the situation. Get your child involved in making the bite better, perhaps by getting a cold compress to put on it and asking them to help. If the biting becomes persistent, it is probable that their urge to bite is overwhelming and they are unable to resist. In this case, offer them alternatives to bite on such as a wooden brick or an apple.

Biting can make parents feel very awkward in social situations, but it is likely that other parents in your group have or will experience this behaviour at some point. Talk to them about it and make it clear that you are aware and dealing with it.

As with all of the subjects I discuss in this book, the most difficult aspect of parenting your child gently through them, is often the knowledge that you are being watched and judged by others. People want to know that you are doing your job, and unfortunately, most people expect or hope to see a punishment. Talking to these parents gives you the opportunity to show them that you are not being permissive, and you are indeed parenting your child through these situations.

It is easy to feel as if it is none of their business, and that you shouldn't have to explain yourself to them, but in taking the time to talk through your methods you will be bridging a gap and showing respect for them and their child.

Talking and sharing information educates and informs others that there are different ways of parenting and dealing with behaviour, that do not involve punishments. So many parents are stuck in a cycle of punishments and bribery and don't know what to do to break away from it. Watching these situations being handled with love and fairness can give an insight into a different way. Their own families may benefit hugely from your insights. Be honest and remain confident in your decision to parent with respect for your child.

CHAPTER 9

My toddler won't eat!

It is actually quite common for toddlers to lose interest in food. After the initial interest during the weaning onto solids phase, this sudden decrease in appetite can cause concern to their parents. This is the time when the dinner time battles begin, with the toddler firmly asserting their autonomy, whilst the parent tries every trick in their tool box to get their child to eat something. From bribery to punishment, whatever they try just does not work.

Of course if you look at this situation from the toddlers point of view, it is very frustrating and annoying to be forced away from what they are doing to be coaxed into eating, when they just don't feel hungry. In focusing so much attention onto the situation, it creates a pressure around mealtimes that inevitably, makes the child distance themselves even further from food as they start to associate it with unhappy times.

Most of the time, if left to their own devices, children will eat when their body needs it. The problem we have is that this is usually a lot less than we have become accustomed to expect. We are fed (pun intended!) an image of a healthy toddler devouring three meals a day plus snacks, but is this realistic? Surely a much more sensible option is to let the child eat when they are hungry? After all, don't we know ourselves when we need to eat, from the rumble in our stomach and our thoughts turning to food. Why can't we afford the same trust in our child's bodily signals?

Many adults these days have unhealthy relationships with eating, and some of these can be traced back to our own childhoods. If we were coaxed into clearing our plate, and bribed with desert or threat of punishment, we may have long forgotten to listen to our own bodily signals, instead just completing the task of filling and emptying our plates at the appropriate times. This might be a good time to copy the eating habits of our children, learning once again to trust our body, and eat when we are hungry, stopping once we are full.

So what can you do if your child just won't eat?

First, have a good look at them. Do they look healthy or are they wasting away? Your instincts should be enough to tell you if your child is seriously unwell, and if you believe that to be the case then you should seek medical advice. However, more likely, you will see a child full of energy, healthy and alert.

If this is the situation, start by eliminating the pressure around eating. A great idea is to create family rituals around mealtimes. Light candles, involve your children in setting the table and choosing the music to listen to. This gives them notice that mealtime is about to happen, so they won't be suddenly jolted out of their activities.

As much as possible, involve your child in every step of the process, beginning with going together to buy your food, inviting him to smell and feel the vegetables and place them into the trolley, continuing the journey when you get home by getting him involved in unpacking and putting items into the fridge.

Then when it is time to cook, have him peel, chop, stir, with your assistance until he is proficient in each area. Getting your child involved in the whole process from start to finish will be far more interesting for him, than just having his dinner plonked in front of him.

If you have the inclination, growing your own vegetables and fruit is another wonderful activity that your toddler can be involved in.

The excitement and anticipation of watching each plant grow until the day you can pick it from the soil and take it to the pot, is a great way of sparking an interest in food.

But what if you do all this and they still don't eat I hear you cry! Show your child how it's done. The table is set, the dinner is cooked, now sit down and enjoy your meal. Invite your child to join you at the table to eat, but if they refuse to eat anything (or even refuse to come and sit down!) just relax. Don't be pushy about it, you will only make eating seem like a chore. Keep it fun and stress free and you can rest assured that in time, they will want to join in with the family meals.

Here are some things you can do in the meantime though.

Eat together

This might be a bit of work rethinking what time you have dinner, or what time everyone goes to bed, but do what you can to ensure you have at least one meal a day with the whole family. Try to ensure that your child always has company when they eat their other meals through the day, to role model healthy eating. Again, keep it fun, stress free and voluntary.

Serve the same food to the whole family

Creating a meal is a big job and taking on different food orders from each person is stressful and time consuming. Take into account dislikes and preferences, but don't be afraid to serve something your child says she doesn't like.

Children's taste buds are constantly evolving and she may try it and decide it tastes good after all. Make sure it is only a small part of the dish so she has the option to take it or leave it without going hungry, and of course, don't pressurise anyone to eat something they don't want.

Walk the talk, it's no good serving a healthy meal to your child while you tuck into a takeaway and huge dessert. Occasional treats are different, but if your everyday diet is lacking in nutrients, you need to get on board with healthy eating too.

Forget strict rules about when and where it's OK to eat

Lay out plates of healthy snacks that can be picked at throughout the day, and carry snacks with you so you are ready when they ask. If the snacks you have in stock are healthy and nutritious, it won't matter if they ask for one thirty minutes before a mealtime. Worry less about when they should eat and let their body decide for them. Let your toddler sit at a big chair on a cushion next to you if they hate their high-chair, or set out a picnic in the garden.

Share your own food if it seems more appealing to them

This one is something that parents often struggle with as they don't want to encourage bad habits. They are concerned that their child will never eat independently if they are allowed to eat from the parents plate. I have several points to make on the matter. Number one, WHO CARES! Why is it so important that everyone gets their own plate? This again stems back to our own childhoods and our own food issues. There is enough for every-body, so relax and just let go of what meal time "should" look like.

My second point is that by releasing your boundaries and sharing your food with love and without resentment, you are modelling the best example for your child, in the art of shar-ing. As I discussed in the chapter Mine, yours and ours – Toddlers can share, not many tod-dlers want to give up what they have, as they are taught from very early on *This is mine, that is yours.* It's little wonder they hold on strong to whatever they have. By smashing these conventional rules of possession, your child will happily share whatever he has with you.

Lastly, sharing food is very intimate and a wonderful bonding experience. Some of my happiest memories are of sitting in a park shar-ing a sandwich with my son, or passing an apple back and forth.

Keep the food options healthy

Many parents, in a state of desperation give cakes or unhealthy fast foods to their child, with the idea that at least they are eating some-thing, which has to be better than nothing. My tip is to keep the foods in your home varied and interesting, but also entirely healthy. If they fill up on chocolate or fried chips, they have even less reason to eat the healthy stuff later. Toddlers don't know about these un-healthy food options yet, and you will be do-ing them a big favour if you establish healthy eating habits and food choices while they are young.

For parents who say *"But she won't eat any-thing but chicken nuggets!"* I have to be harsh and say, that's because you give them to her. These foods are salty, sugary and so far from their natural state. They are addictive and chil-dren who have been given such foods regu-larly will have developed a taste for them, so other foods seem bland and tasteless. Replace the rubbish with nutritious food and sooner or later, their taste for good food will return and they will devour it.

Buy yourself a juicer!

You can make delicious and sweet tasting, all

natural organic juices, which are full to the brim with nutrients, fibre and vitamins. Again, involve your child in sourcing the fruit and vegetables for the juice and make it a fun experience, having a rewarding drink together every day. You can add spinach and dark green vegetables to your juices, and adding apples will sweeten the taste.

You may be surprised to find that the more refreshing green juices go down just as well as the sweeter fruit ones. Bananas make a delicious smoothie texture which tends to be popular with toddlers, and adding a coconut based milk is also a great way to make a fun milkshake! It may be a bit difficult encouraging your toddler to try the juice in the first place but once they taste it, they will likely find it irresistible in the future. Instead of pushing them to taste your creation, enjoy the juices as a family, and ask your little one to take a glass through to Daddy/Mummy. By the time it reaches them it will most likely be all gone!

CHAPTER 10

Breastfeed them! Breastfeeding through the toddler stage

My final tip, and one deserving of its own chapter is to breastfeed. This is my most valuable advice. If you are still breastfeeding and considering if you should stop, my advice is simply – don't.

Breastfeeding your child gives you the confidence that although your toddler is not eating much, they are still filling up on all those incredible breast milk nutrients. It is also very reassuring if your child is not keen on drinking fluids from a cup either.

There are many, many reasons to continue breastfeeding your child through toddlerhood and further still. Contrary to some beliefs, the nutritional benefits are still high, and the longer you breastfeed, the lower your risk of breast cancer and ovarian cancer. You still get that wonderful boost of oxytocin when you feed, which will help you in feeling joyful and bonded, even on those difficult days.

Your toddler will benefit from a stronger immune system, higher IQ, as well as lower risk of obesity, cholesterol and high blood pressure in the future. Along with this they will also benefit from the greater security, bonding and comfort that comes with full term breastfeeding.

Often when a parent is considering whether she should bring the breastfeeding relationship to a close, she is not actually sure of her own reasons for stopping, instead feeling completely overwhelmed by the reasons of others. Perhaps it is because the accepted societal norm for ceasing nursing is looming, it may be outside pressure from family members or friends, the feeling that she has to teach her child to be independent of her, to sleep without assistance, or simply that it has to come to an end at some point so why not now.

But, many mothers who stop, do so with great sadness for the wonderful breastfeeding relationship that is over. When they dig deep into their true feelings on the subject, many would say that they were not ready to stop. The same is true for their child. For a toddler who has always had free access to the breast, it can be difficult to understand why they are no longer allowed to seek comfort from nursing. Weaning can feel sudden and forced, and this can affect the behaviour of the toddler, and the relationship and trust between mother and child.

Throughout the world there are many children who have free access to the breast until they naturally wean from nursing. Although even during a natural weaning process, the end may still be sad, it is tackled together, mother and child in partnership. Both their needs are being met through the breastfeeding relationship, and they are not at war or in conflict with one another.

Children will naturally wean from breastfeeding with no input or planning from the mother typically anywhere from two to eight years old.

If weaning is something you are sure you need to do, beginning a gentle process of offering more solid food and a cup of water may help speed the weaning process up without a lot of stress for both parties. But if you do decide to stick with it, you will find there are huge benefits to nursing a toddler.

As stated earlier, you are safe in the knowledge that your child is regularly taking on a nutritious and calorie laden snack. They are also keeping hydrated at regular intervals throughout the day.

In addition to this, breastfeeding helps you to reconnect and tune in to each other during an otherwise busy day. It enables you to have that special one on one time to focus on one another. It soothes an overtired, over excited toddler, on the verge of a meltdown. It works as a distraction when you have had to be firm in setting boundaries. It resets the mood when everything seems to be getting out of control.

And on top of all that, there is nothing quite like seeing the joy your child still gets from nursing. Knowing that they feel entirely safe, comforted and nourished from your milk is an unbeatable feeling. Breastfeeding will see you through the toddler phase and prove to be the most reliable tool in your kit.

A note for mothers who are not lactating

Breastfeeding is the optimal milk for your toddler. However, if you have already stopped breastfeeding, or never did it in the first place, there are still many ways you can be responsive to your child's needs. Formula fed children often fall into a pattern of feeding, so the parent can learn to expect the next feed. This leads many to become rigid in the routine and firm clock watchers. But it is important to remember, these are children we are talking about, not machines, not robots. They need their parent to be flexible and to listen to them, and see their needs. Their little bodies are going through continuous developments, and their emotional development is just as important.

Breastfeeding is so much more than a meal. It is comfort, security and love. Try to mirror these qualities in your own feeding rituals. Have open and welcoming arms without reservation, and provide comfort in other ways, singing, reading and snuggling together.

CHAPTER 11

Dealing with strong emotions

I'm going to start this chapter by saying I really dislike the term "tantrum." If any other human was to display the kind of behaviours associated with tantrums, they would be described quite differently. Words such as distraught, devastated, exhausted, overwhelmed, unwell, or frustrated would most likely be used. These words are also the best choice when a toddler is expressing their strong feelings.

The very act of saying *"She is just having a tantrum,"* usually said with a roll of the eyes and a shared *"tut"* between the adults, distances us from our children. It creates a barrier, and feelings of annoyance and anger emerge on the parents side. By choosing to look further to see not just what a child is doing, but instead, why they are doing it and how they are feeling, we can approach the situation calmly with love and acceptance, no matter what.

A common issue parents face, is that their child begins to show signs of stress and begins to shout, scream, refuse help or instruction, and we in turn find ourselves becoming stressed and worked up. This creates a spiral effect, our heightened emotions then cause our child to become even more agitated and this is when meltdowns occur.

If we remain calm, this doesn't need to happen. But first you have to free up your own self conscious feelings, know that it is perfectly natural for your child to sometimes have difficulty expressing their emotions, for the simple reason that their brains are not yet developed enough to cope with these feelings. This will help you to keep your cool, even when passers by are watching or offering suggestions and advice.

> You have nothing to be embarrassed about and it is not your job to make your child be quiet and compliant. Your job is to be there for your child and help them to work through these emotions.

Let me give you a personal example

Myself, my husband and our seventeen month old son were out walking in the woods, my son riding in the sling on my husband's back.

At some point along the walk, he decided that he wanted to get down from the sling, so down he came. Only, he didn't want to walk, so instead, we stopped and relaxed on the grass for a while enabling our son to explore the area. After we had been there for a while we got up to go and he walked for a little while. But he was starting to get tired and kept sitting down. He didn't want to walk. He refused to go back in the sling, and each time I picked him up he screamed and tried to get down, where he would promptly throw himself onto the ground and cry.

Knowing my son and his usual habits, I knew he was feeling hot and tired and that he didn't know how to deal with these feelings. I also knew that we couldn't resolve this without getting back to the car for him to be able to have a sleep out of the heat.

He was sitting on the path and in danger of being knocked down by a cyclist, so I picked him up. He screamed and kicked. I remained calm. Very quietly and gently I sang a familiar song as we walked, and he continued to cry. We were approaching a huge tree and one of our family rituals is to lay our hands on the largest trees to feel their energy and ground ourselves. My little boy always greets them with *"Hello tree"* when we do this. So, continuing to hold him and sing, I freed up one hand and lay it on the tree. We stood there like that for a minute as his cries went from desperate to entirely subsided, and then he looked up and quietly said *"Hello tree."*

This worked not only as a distraction for him, but as a calming measure for me. I didn't get stressed, I didn't get embarrassed, and I was there for my son while he struggled with his feelings. Once he was calm, I continued to carry him through the woods, talking to him in the same gentle tones about what had happened.

I voiced his feelings for him (those that I could see), telling him *"You are feeling hot and tired, we are going back to the car so you can sleep."* After a few more minutes he was happy to go back in the sling, and we made it back with no further incidents.

* * *

There is no doubt that going from the baby stage into toddlerhood can be difficult on us parents. Where before, you could pick your baby up and take them to where you needed to be, now you may face a meltdown by repeating the same action. One reason for this is that your baby is no longer an extension of your body, no longer happy to watch your every action. They are becoming more independent and have their own ideas about what they would like to do. When you pick them up and carry them away from an activity, no matter how nicely you do it, or how much warning you give them, the fact is that you are interfering with them. You may be interrupting what they were doing or what they had been exploring, or maybe they are simply frustrated at your ability to swoop them away at your whim.

Think about the times when your child is likely to struggle with their emotions. The most common causes are tiredness, hunger, being too hot or cold, over stimulation, boredom, not enough freedom to explore, and new, potentially scary situations.

As a parent there is a lot you can do to make things easier on both yourself and your toddler. Carry snacks and drinks with you, breastfeed on cue, don't skip naps. If your child won't sleep in a sling or buggy, try not to make plans for when they will be needing to nap, or instead, create a quiet and relaxing space where they can rest peacefully whilst you are out.

My top tips for parenting toddlers through these strong emotions, are distraction, discussion and creating a safe and unrestricted environment for them to live in. Toddlers have a strong need to explore and investigate their surroundings and one of the most frustrating things a parent can do, is constantly tell them "No," or move them away from what they are exploring. A far better solution is to get rid of anything dangerous or breakable that you are uncomfortable with them playing with.

Cover your electricity sockets, move your chemicals out of reach, and store away anything precious. Then back off. Yes they will climb, yes they will open drawers and pull things out and yes they will sometimes make a mess or bump their heads. But these are all learning experiences.

* * *

Around the world different cultures have different ways of reacting to tantrums. The Inuit have a belief that when a baby is born, it takes on the spirit of a recently deceased relative. This means that instead of being treated like "a baby" in western terms, they are given the same respect that the deceased adult would have been given. Not only does this lead to the child being given more freedom in deciding when they are hungry or tired, which is a positive thing for a child, but it also means the child is left to experience their emotions without interference or placating.

A passage from "The Inuit way" reads:

"These beliefs regarding children have resulted in Inuit parents allowing their children a much greater degree of freedom than most non-Inuit would be comfortable with. As long as they do not harm themselves, other people, or damage important items such as food or hunting equipment, there are few limits placed on the activities of children. This should not be interpreted as the parents being overly permissive, because the practice includes certain limitations as well.

For example, a child may receive affectionate cuddling or choice bits of food when he requests it, however, a child who is pouting or throwing a tantrum may be ignored. To do otherwise would be considered intrusive and would possibly slow the development of the child's ability to reason. A large amount of freedom does not mean that Inuit children are not disciplined. Young children will be restrained if they persist in a potentially dangerous activity. Subtle verbal clues by older members of the family indicate to the child when their behaviour is inappropriate."

A section from an article entitled Child Raising In Non-violent Cultures, Creating a culture that chooses non-violence with intention reads:

"For most... non-violent cultures, adult behaviour with children from ages two or three is usually not quite so permissive as for infants, but child aggressive behaviour is still met with generally non-aggressive adult controls such as interruption rather than physical punishment. Among the ! Kung Bushmen of south west Africa, Patricia Draper describes three general adult responses: when the child's aggression is toward a younger child, the aggressor is scolded harshly; if toward a peer, the children are distracted or separated if necessary; if toward an adult, the behaviour is usually ignored.

I have seen a seven-year-old crying and furious, hurling sticks, nut shells, and eventually burning embers at her mother. The mother sat at her fire talking with the child's grandmother and her own sister-in-law. Bau (the mother) put up her arm occasionally to ward off the thrown objects but carried on her conversation nonchalantly. The other women remained unperturbed despite the hail of missiles. The daughter raged ten feet away, but Bau did not turn a hair. When the rocks and nut shells came close Bau remarked, "That child has no brains."

This example is not an isolated case but a common practice. Adults consistently ignore a child's angry outburst when it does not inflict harm. A child's frustration at such times is acute, but he learns that anger does not cause an adult to change his treatment of the child, and the display of anger does not get the adult's attention or sympathy. In these situations the reward to the child for hostile acts must be minimal. The child can rage until he is tired, but, in my observation, the tirade had little effect.

The children from these cultures are cooperative rather than competitive, and nurturant rather than domineering in their relationships with one another. "

These excerpts present an interesting viewpoint on the different ways that tantrums are handled in non-violent cultures, and I think it is worth remembering that these parents have not had the onslaught of parenting advice and expert "studies" we in the west have had pushed on us. As such, their thoughts are not clouded with the advice of others, and they will be likely parenting much closer to their basic human instincts. However I believe that between the typical western attitudes of getting angry and punishing a tantrum, or conversely pandering and bargaining with their child, and the opposite end of the scale shown in these passages, of completely ignoring the outburst, there is a middle ground that neither rewards nor dismisses a child having a meltdown.

A child having a tantrum is experiencing some overwhelming emotions, possibly for the first time. Once they become sucked into this vortex of emotions it can become very difficult to reason with them. They will feel frightened, lost in their feelings and possibly fixated with the cause of this upset, which to the parents mind, can be something very insignificant.

> To ignore a child going through this, can create confusion and more fear and anger within the child. This can lead to an even bigger meltdown causing more stress to both the child and the parents.

As a parent you know your child best. Sometimes any sort of involvement on your part when your child is in the beginning stages of a tantrum, can escalate and encourage the situation to become much more heated and violent than necessary. Often simply continuing with your activity whilst standing your ground on your boundaries, can be the quickest way for the child to accept the way the situation is, and for their anger to fizzle out. However, although you may not necessarily stop what you are doing, it is important to stay in tune with your child and the situation. This gives you the advantage of being able to see when, rather than dissipating, the tantrum is becoming more heated and your child is loosing control. This is your opportunity to step in and work through the emotions with your child before they reach their crisis point.

To try to bribe and plead with them to be quiet, or punish them for being "unreasonable and naughty" is missing the point entirely. Learning to experience and cope with these emotions is a natural part of a child's development, and to expect a child to have a handle on them without any guidance and support from a loving adult, is completely illogical.

So let's look at the middle ground. A parent here knows that it is important to stay with their child during these emotional struggles. This parent knows their child well, and can see when a situation is turning from a mild upset or frustration, into a place of fear and a potential tantrum. When this happens they will step in and gently work through these feelings together, voicing the child's emotions, silently seeking out unmet needs such as tiredness, and offering alternative solutions or

perhaps just a helping hand to aid the toddler in their endeavours. In doing this, the majority of potential tantrums will be avoided before they even begin. However, there may be times where it all gets too much.

Boundaries and safety measures are in place for a reason, and as gentle as you may be in helping a child to understand this, flexibility is not an option here. If after doing all of the things above your child is still unable to cope with the situation, and it spirals into a melt-down, there are several steps you can take to ensure that the stress is as minimal as possible for both of you, and that the situation is de-es-calated with respect for your child's feelings.

Firstly, keep calm. Know that this is not an attack on you or a method of manipulation. Take some deep breaths and assert yourself as the adult. You have an important role to guide and support your child through this, and it will not help either of you if you become stressed and angry, getting on an equal level with your child's emotions and having a tan-trum of your own. You need to be their anchor. So step back and see the situation as it really is. A frightened child with an unmet need, unable to process the situation they have found them-selves in. This will give you the patience to em-pathise and be there for them through this time.

Secondly, respect your child and their feel-ings. It may seem ridiculous that they are so upset over something so small, but don't belittle their feelings. If it is important to them than that should be good enough for you. Getting frustrated about it won't help.

Thirdly, stay with them at all times. This is not something that should be seen as an inconvenience, nor something to laugh about with passers by. This is your relationship, your child, their trust in you. It is a time to prove that you will be there through the good times and the bad and that you love them no matter what.

And lastly, use gentle tones to talk through their feelings. Explain gently but firmly why a particular boundary is necessary. If they will allow you to touch them, come in close and hold them through the storm.

> Periodically offer a cuddle, hold their hand and keep your own arms open and welcoming.

Use repetitive soothing phrases such as *"I know you feel sad,"* and rub their back or stroke their hair until they are feeling more relaxed.

A great tool to use to bring an emotional

struggle to an abrupt close is breastfeeding. This can work as a reset button and calm a heated situation down, but it is important that even if the child becomes immediately calm once latched on, the parent still takes the time to gently talk them through what happened and what they were feeling, so they may learn the words to describe their emotions in the future.

Once the child is calm, tell them exactly what is happening next and give them a distraction. Some examples are:

"We are going back to our house now, can you carry your doll?"

"It's time for bed now, do you want to come and choose a story?"

"Daddy is going to work now, let's wave goodbye from the door."

If there is a need that you have pinpointed during the meltdown such as tiredness or hunger, make it your priority to meet it as soon as possible, to make your child comfortable and prevent another emotional struggle.

And remember, this is such a short period in their life. Supporting your child through a tantrum is not (as many fear) encouraging them to be dramatic and demanding in the long run. You can be firm in your boundaries alongside parenting gently through a meltdown.

With your love and guidance, your child will learn much more quickly how to voice and cope with these strong emotions, and come out of the toddler stage with a belief that they are never alone. This ability to rely on you to support them rather than punish or ignore them, provides the foundations to a strong parent child relationship, enabling you to cope with future childhood and adolescent issues as a team, instead of with conflict.

The early years are not always easy, but following your instincts and meeting your child's needs is the best thing you can do for yourself and for your child.

CHAPTER 12

The huge disadvantages to
the time out method

I'm going to assume you have heard of a discipline technique known as time out. The technique is popular on television programmes such as Supernanny and Nanny 911, and is now so accepted that people rarely stop to question its effects. However, time outs are not only NOT a guaranteed path to success (hence the need to administer them repeatedly for the same behaviours) but they also damage the natural respect and connection between parent and child.

A time out is a parent enforced consequence, where a child is usually put in a particular spot. The accepted term which I truly dislike is the "naughty spot" for an allotted amount of time. This is usually the number of minutes equal to the child's age, e.g. five minutes for a five year old.

The child would receive a warning that if their behaviour continues they will go on the spot, and if they then repeat the behaviour, they are forcibly taken to the spot, told the reason for why they have been put there, then left alone to sit and think about what they have done. If they move at all from the spot, they are taken back to it and their time starts all over again. When they have completed their allotted time, they are told once more why they were put on the spot, and asked to say they are sorry. If they refuse to say they are sorry, they have to do the time out again. This is repeated as many times as the parent deems necessary, until the child apologises. Until the next time...

The disadvantages of time outs are catastrophic in terms of your relationship with your child. The use of them encourages our children to lie to us in order to avoid being punished. What incentive do they have to explain what happened and how they are feeling, if they know they are going to have to sit on the naughty step wasting their time?

Not only that, but how long will it take for them to learn that the word "sorry" is their get out of jail free card? But, when used as a bargaining tool, how likely is it that they will truly grasp the meaning of the word, or have any real feelings or remorse behind its use?

Forcibly moving a child to the spot tends to go one of two ways. One is that the child loves this new found game and attention, finds it hilarious to run from the spot the instant they are put there, and makes a total laughing stock of the parent as they chase back and forth after them, loosing all semblance of respect along the way. In this scenario, the child enjoys the one to one time so much, that although it is all negative attention, they grasp on to it and end up breaking their parents rules far more frequently, just so they can play this ridiculous game.

The other side of the coin is that the child refuses to sit on the naughty spot, and the parent chooses to repeatedly bring them back to prove their point. The child becomes more and more distressed, crying, screaming and kicking out. They are no longer in any frame of mind to understand why they are being put there, or why they are being treated this way by the person who loves them most in this world. The parent continues the chase, sometimes persevering for hours on end, repeating the action of bringing them back to the spot, all the while ripping apart the trust that their child has in them that they are on their side.

The effects of this process are almost equal to leaving a child to cry it out. I have heard of people using this technique from as young as one year old! In this instance, the child shuts down and you lose the vital connection that is in fact, the best tool for coping with difficult situations and disagreements between parents and children.

If time outs are already part of your behaviour management strategies and you have realised how damaging they are, don't despair that it is too late to regain your connection. It will take a lot of work on your part to regain the trust your child has in you, but you need to believe that you both deserve so much better in life. Start rebuilding that trust now.

CHAPTER 13

Say you're Sorry!

How often do we hear this? A child has hurt someone or taken their toy and the parent tells them to, *"Say you're sorry!"* This is an approach that many parents use, and although I agree that children need to learn to recognise the affect their actions have on others, I don't think a forced apology actually teaches the desired lesson.

Let me tell you a little story:

A two year old boy I once cared for, started to become rough with the other children in the group. His parents, shocked by his behaviour made a big issue of it, and after each incident they witnessed, insisted that he say he was sorry and give the other child a hug. He was quite adorable giving his apology and everyone was very happy that he had learned his lesson.

Well, he had learned a lesson but it wasn't the one his parents had hoped for. What he had learned was that he could be as rough as he liked, take people's things, break things on purpose and all he had to do was say sorry afterwards. Before long he didn't even have to be asked. He would run over to another child and grab them by the hair, pull them to the floor and before anyone had even had time to react, he would turn and sweetly say *"sorry"* and run off to the next thing. It put everyone in a very difficult position, he had apologised so that was that, wasn't it? His parents didn't know what else to do, as it felt wrong to take it any further since he had acknowledged his mistake.

The fact is, saying the word does not equate to feeling the emotion. That is something that takes years to learn, and toddlers don't always see that they have caused hurt to someone. In the early years, the world revolves around them and the concept of "sorry" is just too big to understand without being able to observe it in action.

Children will learn to say they are sorry under their own steam if they are given the opportunity to witness others remedying their own mistakes, and saying sorry themselves.

If you as their parent say something hurtful

to another adult, or react unfairly to your child's behaviour, show them that it is not a weakness to apologise and recognise your own mistakes.

It takes humility and courage to say you were wrong, but in doing so not only will it show your child that you feel bad for your behaviour, but it will also show them that it's OK to admit you were wrong.

We must also remember that apologies do not always come in the form of words. Often our children will feel sad or guilty for their actions, and will remedy them in their own unique way. They may watch carefully to ensure the other person is OK, they may offer them a toy they have found, or a gentle pat on the arm. They may ask an adult if the wronged party is alright. They can make their feelings of concern known, without the situation becoming one of force and coercion as an adult attempts to get them to say something they just aren't comfortable with. It can be difficult and exposing to say those words out loud, especially if they are being watched by what they perceive as a disapproving audience, and it may be that your child just isn't ready to take that step.

> If we stop looking for the words and instead start seeing their attempts at remedying the situation, we may find that they *have* acknowledged the effect their actions had on the other person, and that they are indeed empathising with their sorrow.

This is an opportunity to take your child aside for a calming one to one talk, using blame free language to discuss what happened. It doesn't have to become complicated. Simply stating which action triggered which result and how it could be handled differently next time can be enough to reinforce the message within their mind. Keeping anger and blame towards the child out of the situation, and instead focusing on the action rather than the child herself, will prevent her from feeling attacked and shutting off completely.

Helping children to care about others can be done in a multitude of ways, and often it can be easier for a toddler to express themselves in actions rather than words. If it appears that they want to make amends but don't know how, here is a good opportunity for you to step in with a few gentle suggestions of your own. Some examples are, giving them a cloth to wipe up a spill, offering them a cold flannel or a drink to give to an injured child, or asking for their help in tidying up an area. This should be offered up as a choice so that they don't feel forced or pressurised into it, which would only serve to build resentment. Instead, in freely choosing to accept your suggestion, they will feel empowered and able to wipe the slate clean if they are holding on to any un-comfortable feelings of guilt.

CHAPTER 14

The Truth about Physical Punishment

Although it is now widely recognised that smacking is an unacceptable thing to do to a child, it is still also widely used as a means of control and punishment. One of the reasons for this is our cultural ties. We learn how to parent from our own parents, and the way we were treated as children will have had a deep effect on each of us. In our parents generation, following on from Victorian practices, hitting children was far more accepted.

It is very easy for us to blame our own parents for smacking us in our childhoods, however, we must remember how different things were for them when we were children. There was no internet, very little in the way of support or attachment parenting groups. Our parents most likely had no role models other than their own parents to learn from. Most would have experienced the cane at school, frequent smacks or even whippings.

Although their own instincts may have felt jarred by this form of discipline, in a desperation to have a "good child" they may have felt that they had no choice. I am not saying that what they did was right, only that it was almost inevitable that the cycle of violence continued through the generations. Luckily for us we are in a time where we have a multitude of information just a few clicks away on the world wide web. There are support groups everywhere, and natural and attachment parenting are being rediscovered in all their beauty.

> We have the opportunity to break the cycle and protect the generations to come.

So what's the problem with physical punishment anyway?

Smacking, spanking, hitting, whatever people term it, all boils down to one thing – Causing some sort of pain, either physical or emotional (but usually both), to a child.

I recently saw a newspaper clipping from the 1950s talking about the circumstances when it was acceptable to hit a woman. The overall response was that if the woman is not behaving as the husband deems fit, she is asking for a whack. This view nowadays would cause a shocked response and provoke outrage. A man who used physical punishment on his wife to get her to behave a certain way, or more likely as a release of his anger, would be arrested. So why is it that people still turn a blind eye to a parent who smacks? I know many, many people disagree with this argument, countering that it is different to smack a child, they are still learning and need guidance. But let's look at the effects.

If a man beats his wife, she is likely to feel frightened, hurt, ashamed, resentful, angry, helpless and of course pain. She will lose the trust she has in her man to protect her and love her unconditionally. Now let's compare that to how a child feels when his parent hits him. Frightened, hurt, ashamed, resentful, angry, helpless, pain and broken trust. It doesn't matter what your justification is, a human being is a human being no matter what their age.

They will still feel all the same feelings, the only difference being that a child is stuck in that situation. They have no option of leaving and no one to confide in.

When parents use physical punishment, they are usually trying to control a child's behaviour in some way. But in exerting their power over a child and conjuring up all of these feelings of despair, they are creating sides. You are no longer on their side and that is very clear. Why should they listen to you, when you won't listen to them?

Either one of two things will happen. The child, so petrified of what might happen to them, loses all sense of autonomy and becomes a robot answering to your every demand. Think that's what you want out of your child? See chapter three - Moving away from control, towards guidance.

Alternatively, they rebel. They not only repeat the behaviour, but they also become skilled at lying to you, concealing their true selves, closing themselves off to you and finding people they can trust in their peers. Their influences then come from the people they spend the most time with, which in our society is typically friends around their own age.

Although we know that physical punishment does not lead to peaceful parenting, simply educating ourselves on the reasons to avoid it is just not enough.

This is why many parents start out with good intentions, with the idea that they won't be anything like their own parents, but a few years down the line, find themselves overcome with rage or an urge to smack and shout. To change this behaviour, we need to go further than seeking information. We need to completely reprogramme our whole psychology, replacing our old outdated instincts with new ones. We need to analyse our reactions to challenging situations and rewire our automatic response.

It is OK to WANT to smack your child. Does that statement surprise you? Then let me explain my meaning. The urge to smack your child, is simply down to your instincts to parent as your own parents did. It may be very difficult for you to distance yourself from this urge when you encounter stressful parenting situations.

The key is to recognise these feelings, accept them and consider *why* you are experiencing them. Then you can begin to work on changing them.

Wanting to smack does not make you a bad person. It speaks of your own childhood and past experiences. Recognising that you want to do things differently is your first positive step.

So what can you do if you have already begun using some form of physical punishment on your child. The very first step is to arm yourself with all of the information to back up the damaging effects of smacking, spanking and so on. Make a solemn vow to yourself that you will never touch your child in punishment or anger, ever again. Plan what you are going to do when you encounter a stressful situation with your child, and go over and over this plan in your head to prevent you from acting in the heat of the moment. The chapter Alternatives to traditional discipline will give you some methods to use.

Next, sit down with your child. Explain to them that you know you were wrong to smack them, and you are very sorry for what you have done. Tell them that whatever has happened was not their fault and you love them so much, and you will never hurt them again. It doesn't matter how much they understand this communication. They deserve to hear it and you deserve to have a clean slate. Living with guilt is harmful and soul destroying. Make a promise to your child that you will never do it again. Then start afresh. Children so desperately want an unconditional love and connection from their parents. It is never too late to start making the right choices.

CHAPTER 15

Alternatives to traditional discipline

So you may be reading along here, agreeing with me on the subject of avoiding time outs and physical punishments, but trying to work out what you can do instead. Although I am not keen on the dictatorial style of parenting, I am not suggesting permissiveness either. Children need a strong and self assured role model to guide them in the ways of the world, and ignoring and endorsing behaviours that are inappropriate is not the way to go. Balance, boundaries and flexibility are the key ingredients to successful parenting.

A household of unbreakable rules (is there such a thing?) is asking for trouble and rebellion. So, she did something you asked her not to do? What about the circumstances surrounding the event? Our reaction to this type of situation boils down to our learned habits of punishment from society, and also our own childhoods: *"She should learn a lesson here."*

In a fair household, mistakes are treated as just that, and there is no need for punishment. It is assumed that the child had no harmful intentions as they are loving and social beings. Instead, punishments and reprimands are replaced with conversation, empathy and understanding.

Putting household routines in place is a great way to get your children on board and involved in family life. I can't stress enough here that having routines does not mean forcing your child into doing anything. For example, if you like a tidy house and one of your routines is to put the toys away before you eat dinner or before you go out, by all means go ahead and do it. Tell your children what you are doing and why, ask them for their help, and pass them things to put away. But if they don't feel like it, let it be. In time, by staying consistent with your routines, and asking (not demanding) them to help, your child will join in of their own choice. But until then, if it is important to you, just do it yourself and remember to find the joy in all that you do.

If your children see you happy and smiling as you go about your work, they will be far more likely to want to get involved too.

If you are stressed and clearly hating every minute of the process, why would they want to do it themselves?

There are likely to be a few things in life, that as a parent, you deem non-negotiable. For me these things are:

- We always hold hands when walking by, or crossing a busy road.

- We don't throw glass or damage property.

- Don't turn the gas on the oven on or off.

- Use gentle touch.

These are the constants, but then there will be situations that arise spontaneously, and we have to decide where the boundaries lie in that moment. This takes a certain amount of experimentation to figure out how to meet everyone's needs.

For example, once when we were in the supermarket my son asked if he could push the trolley. This involved me holding him in my arms as he leaned forward to push it along. It was fun for him, but after a while I began to struggle holding two stone of toddler whilst trying to steer and shop. We were crashing into things and I was no longer enjoying the game, so I said that it was time for him to get down. He wanted to continue pushing, and couldn't cope with my reasoning for ruining this wonderful game.

I gave him several options: go in the sling, sit in the trolley, walk and push the trolley from the side, but none were acceptable to him. This situation got more and more heated until I had to abandon the shopping entirely, and get out of there. I wondered if his intense reaction to having to stop his game was a one off due to over-tiredness, or perhaps teething, so the next time we went shopping he asked to push again, and when I couldn't hold him any longer and had to put him down, the same thing happened.

I realised that he was not yet able to understand or accept my reasons for ending this game, and to prevent upset and angst for both of us during future trips, some boundaries needed to be put in place.

Next time we went shopping, he asked once

again to push the trolley. Knowing I couldn't hold him the whole way round and would have to cut him off again, I decided to get creative. I told him he could push from the side as he walked along instead. He pointed at the trolley, saying *"Up,"* but knowing I was not comfortable starting something I couldn't continue, I remained firm in this boundary.

"I can't hold you while you push as it hurts Mama's back, and I need to shop. If you want to push, hold on here."

He asked a few more times as we went around the shop, but I made it clear that my decision was final, and he accepted it with no tears, no scene. One day, he will be able to understand that he can do something for a short time, and be able to cope when it comes to an end. We will continue to be open to that, but for now, this solution has opened up new options for him that work for both of us.

Because I only make non-negotiable rules where I deem absolutely necessary (mostly through a need for safety but point three on my list has dual reasons, in a need to feed my family; if the oven is turned off, on, up and down whilst I am trying to cook, dinner gets ruined and no one gets fed!) my child does not feel overly controlled, and is far more likely to listen and accept it when I insist upon something.

That doesn't mean that he is always happy about it, but I am 100% consistent with these boundaries and their consequences, which leaves less room for conflict and frustration.

If he won't hold my hand next to the busy road, he can't walk until we reach the field, beach or somewhere safe.

If he throws glass or breaks something on purpose, it is taken away and I explain why.

If he insists on playing with the gas, he either goes up in the sling, or has to leave the kitchen.

Not negotiable

This is not to say that I hold a grudge or forgo second chances. As I previously mentioned in the chapter, Enabling Independence, if I have to pick him up when we are walking, I walk a short distance and then offer him another chance to walk holding hands.

So even the times where the boundaries are solid, there is always another chance for the toddler to express their freedom, and choose to accept these limited but important boundaries.

The rest of the time, flexibility is a must. Toddlers live in the moment and don't always understand the benefit to things we may consider necessary, such as putting on their wellies or coats before they go outside.

A friend recently told me of a struggle with her daughter. They had been heading out to the supermarket but her child had completely refused to put her shoes on. This escalated to such a conflict that the daughter became inconsolable, and dad had to go to the supermarket alone. Although you may be able to logically talk it through with an older child, a toddler who doesn't want to wear their shoes can't necessarily understand your reasons, and even if they do, they may not agree with them.

This is a familiar situation to a lot of parents, and most parents have similar tales to tell, of a toddlers seemingly unreasonable behaviour and a situation that quickly escalates into an almighty scene! Situations like this require us as the parent to step back and take a deep breath, regain our patience and see the situation for what it really is.

Too often we are drawn into a battle with our children, when from the outsiders point of view, a little creativity and thinking outside the box would have found a solution that met everyone's needs.

So how could this mother have handled this situation differently? She could have held her down and forced her shoes on, which is the conventional response, but where is the trust and respect for her child's wishes in doing that? She could have waited ten minutes and then tried again.

But, the option which would have ticked all the boxes in my mind, is to put her shoes into my bag, carry her to the car so she didn't get soaked in the rain, and go to the supermarket. Once there I would offer the shoes again, as once she can see she is outside, this may feel OK to her. But if she continued to refuse, I would not push the issue. After all, if she really wants to walk barefoot around the supermarket, where is the harm?

These are the things we really need to address within our parenting. Is it really necessary to be non-negotiable on this point? Does it really matter if she won't pick up that toy, or if he gives in to his urge to climb to the top of the sofa?

I hope this idea is not taken as me promoting permissive parenting and the notion that you should never ask anything of your children. I actually ask quite a lot of my son. But asking is very different from demanding. I ask him to bring his bowl to the kitchen when he has finished eating. I ask him to put the dishes away when they are dry, to blow out the candles after dinner, to come and get dressed, to put rubbish in the bin, to bring me my shoes/pen/drink and on and on.

The majority of the time when I ask something of him, he does it. Not only that but he does it with a smile on his face and joy in his heart. He doesn't do it because he has to, as this is simply not the case. He does it because he wants to be a useful member of the family, and he really enjoys being involved in household tasks. He knows that I won't feel any differently about him if he doesn't do it, and he is not helping in order to receive a reward, verbal or otherwise.

I in turn, do things for him when he asks. It's a very balanced relationship and neither one feels like they owe it to the other, or have to give up our own needs to meet those of the other. It's simply cooperation, compromising and serenity.

The parent/child relationships we see in our current society, are often of dictatorial parents and victim children, indulgent parents and spoiled children, neglectful parents and lost children, either sinking into the background or screaming out for attention. But the true parent child relationship should be one of guidance, partnership, learning and growing together as one, rather than pitted against one another. That is where we will find trust in each other, and true joy in our parenting.

Role Modelling

The best way to help your children to grow up

to be respectful, caring and conscientious adults, is to role model these qualities to them. If you are messy, swear, over-eat, bully, or have any other behaviours that are not ideal, your child will copy. How many times have you witnessed a mother shouting at her child to stop shouting? Or smacking a child for hitting a sibling?

> Children will do what you do, not what you tell them to do. It's very simple.

Role modelling can often be done in a way that causes confusion in children. For example, a parent may model how to eat with a fork, only to turn back to their own meal and use their fingers. It is important to be authentic in our role modelling, and not ask things of our children that we are not prepared to do ourselves. Think about what is actually important to you.

Children will learn from imitating you, that some behaviours are appropriate at home, but in a different situation, we may have to behave a certain way. There is no need to enforce something (such as always eating with cutlery) at home, just for those occasions you might go out to eat. That's not real life, unless you yourself keep to those same rules. Relax and be confident that if you are polite, caring, generous, tidy and gentle, these traits will be picked up by your children.

So be authentic in your role modelling, and remember you are being watched and heard, even when you are not intentionally displaying a behaviour you want your child to copy.

A short interlude on the subject of school

Children learn everything from watching and imitating their elders, up until they go to school, (as the majority of children do) at which point they begin to learn from their peers.

Although this is a book on the subject of toddlers, I want to interject here with a note on school. This is the time where you may be considering your options for the future, and as such, I believe this point has a place here.

As I mentioned, if and when children go to school, they begin to take on the ideas and values of their peers and teachers. The younger the child is, the less developed their sense of self, and the more impact these outside influences will have on their beliefs and behaviours. The longer you keep them at home with you, the better chance they will have to develop their own values with your guidance. If they then go to school in the later years, they will be strong enough to stand up for what they know to be right, rather than being influenced by the beliefs of others.

In Sweden, Finland and Denmark children do not start school until they reach the age of seven. In France, Spain and Belgium children start school at six. In the UK, school officially starts at age five, but depending on when their birthday falls, children can begin school as young as four.

This is a huge difference, and yet these students beginning formal education much later are not loosing out academically. Studies have shown that a later start to schooling is not detrimental to a child's intelligence, in fact children generally learn quicker at seven or eight, when they are able to process the environment and information fully. This means they catch up with those who started at four and may even overtake them in terms of understanding and ability. Not only that, but their formative early years will have been spent developing their emotional well being.

Instead of sitting in a classroom, they have likely been able to learn more about the real world, as they accompany their parents on their errands. They have learned their values and morals based on the role modelling of their older family members, and the people who they have spent most of their time with. Their imagination and creativity have been allowed to flow freely as they spend the majority of their time exploring and playing.

Depending on your country, school in its entirety, is actually optional. The benefits of keeping your child at home do not suddenly stop at age seven, and if you have never considered the possibility of home education, world schooling or unschooling, you may find it interesting to look in to these options.

I provide this information not to make you feel guilty, but to share with you that there are many ways of educating, which don't necessarily have to mean going to school. I know that many parents do not have the option of staying at home, but perhaps armed with this information, you may decide to keep your child at home an extra year, enlisting the support of extended family, or maybe you will find a different option for your family. There are many types of schools available and you might find a forest school, or perhaps a smaller Waldorf or Montessori setting that meets your child's needs.

Time In

A wonderful alternative to the time out method, is creating a time in instead. Rather than leaving your child alone to try to process what has happened, and why they are being rejected, instead why not take your child off to a quiet area where the two of you can reflect on the situation together. Sometimes children don't want to be touched or hugged when they reach their limits. During these times, rather than becoming frustrated and walking away, simply sit nearby and give them some time to cry. Remember that their feelings are valid and they have the right to release them by crying and screaming if they need to.

Knowing your child as you do, wait and watch, and when the moment feels right, begin by using soothing tones to talk your child through their feelings. Move closer as you do this, and be open and ready to comfort them in your arms, but don't force a hug on a child who isn't ready. Give them the time they need, whilst remaining constant in your support and love for them.

If and when they are ready for physical comfort, you can reconnect during this time and reflect on what has happened in blame free language. Reassure them that you love them, and empathise with them over what has happened. Use this time to work on strengthening your connection and showing your child that you are always on their side, even when boundaries have been set, or things haven't gone their way. Discuss what provoked the unwanted behaviour and try to come up with a solution that works for everyone. Sometimes a problem won't have a solution, but we can always talk about how this makes them feel and empathise with their struggles.

Hopefully this chapter has given you some

practical ideas to break free from conventional discipline techniques and respond to challenges with a clear head, in a way that meets the whole families needs.

Let's recap the key tools to replace conventional discipline methods:

- Putting household routines and rhythms in place so your child knows what to expect and where they stand.

- Setting firm and necessary boundaries and being clear on your non-negotiables.

- Being consistent in your non-negotiable boundaries and their consequences, and flexible everywhere else.

- Role model in an authentic way i.e. In your real life actions, not just for your toddlers benefit. If you want to make an impact, live your life in a way you can be proud of, and give your children someone worth copying.

- Focus on strengthening your connection to each other and getting to know your child and their triggers, instead of punishing undesirable behaviour.

- Reflect together on the situation, during a "time in" and discuss together your thoughts on why things turned out as they did.

- Be empathetic and understanding of their feelings.

- Find the need behind the behaviour and try to meet it. When you recognise that your child is reaching their limit and is too tired, hungry, overstimulated etc. to cope with the situation facing them, you can pre-empt their behaviour and focus on meeting their need <u>before</u> the behaviour occurs, solving the issue at the source.

CHAPTER 16

Language
and
Labels

Isn't it funny how we all have to be put in a box. It's like we can't relax until we know what category someone fits in to. Most of the words we use to describe others are our own judgement of them, based upon our own standards. Shy, talkative, outgoing, vivacious, naughty, trouble, flirtatious, angry, good, easy going. These are just a few examples of the labels we assign each other.

But what gives us the right to push our evaluations of a persons behaviour onto them? Someone might be labelled as shy and quiet, when in fact he is thoughtful and a listener. Pushing our own words onto another person puts them into a box, and makes them feel they have to live up to (or down to) your standards rather than their own.

When we say a child is naughty for example, we may be describing his actions and his behaviour as not acceptable to our own standards. But in using that word, you are putting him into a box with all sorts of connotations. Instead of directing your dislike towards the particular behaviour, you have instead focused it on the child. His box is full of words and phrases such as, "bad, impossible, a handful, never listens, always does this!" By putting him into this box you are inviting him to prove you right.

Children want to please their parents and meet their expectations. If you are just waiting for him to challenge your rules and disrespect you, he will sense it. If he is called a "naughty boy," then he will try his best *to be* a "naughty boy," for children do not like to disappoint their elders.

So, what about labelling a child good? Will they always be a little angel? Perhaps. But the problem with the word good is that it is generally used to highlight a specific behaviour, *"Oh you are so good for eating all of your dinner." ... "You are so good for doing what I asked."* In the same way that a "naughty" child will feel compelled to keep up the naughty title with their behaviour, a "good" child will need to continue earning their *"good girl"* by continuing to do the things that help them earn the praise.

But what happens when one day they don't feel hungry, or they don't want to stop playing. Should they ignore their own urges in order to please you? If they follow these urges and choose to meet their own needs, they are risking loosing their label. And we grow so used to these labels that they become a part of our identity. A child who has been labelled as good may struggle to find their own motivation to do something for themselves, as they are always looking for that outside validation that they are doing the right thing. It puts an awful lot of pressure on a child to always have to conform to "good."

A more appropriate method would be to focus our attentions inwards, searching for the part of ourself this particular action has struck a chord with, rather than projecting them outwards. So instead of saying:

"You are naughty," you could say *"I felt uncomfortable when you did that."*

Or

"She is so bossy," could be replaced with *"I find it difficult to assert myself in this situation."*

Adults like to highlight children's behaviours whatever they may be, but we can do that without putting any pressure on them to repeat the action. For example, instead of:

"What a good girl for eating your dinner," you could say *"Did you enjoy that meal?"*

Or rather than:

"He is shy," you could say *"He will come to you when he is ready."*

No one likes to be labelled. I have been called shy when I just didn't feel like talking to the person, uncooperative when I didn't agree with a task, fickle when I was finding my feet and exploring my options, and many other labels have been used to try and put me in a box. Have a think about the labels that people have directed at you. Were they accurate or did you feel wrongly assessed?

If we focus more on the present and what is happening right now, we can stop the habit of labelling each other.

Instead of just saying *"She's so moody,"* we

can replace it with real conversation, isolating the issue, finding out the real needs beneath the behaviour, and offering our support instead of our criticism. People worry that in forgoing the labels, their child will miss out on praise and feel that their parents don't care.

Although I think today's children are over praised for things that come naturally, for example eating a meal or defecating in an appropriate spot, I do think that there is a time and a place for praise. When a child creates something they are proud of, when they challenge themselves and try hard, whether they achieve the intended result or not, it is validating for them to hear your praise and support for them. When they overcome their own fears, or spend hours on a project, which they then call you over to see, why should you hold back your pride?

But these are times when a *"Good girl/boy"* just isn't enough. That's not what they want to hear. They want to hear you tell them which part you loved, how you felt so happy for them that they achieved this, they want you to ask questions and actually listen to the answers. They want you to focus your full attention on them and share in their excitement and pride.

That kind of praise is fulfilling and connection building. These times will show that you really are interested in what they are doing, and that you will always make time to listen to them fully. *"Good job,"* or *"Well done,"* gives them very little in terms of meeting their own mood head on. It feels deflating to rush in hoping for *"Wow!"* Hoping for conversation, connection, and bonding, and instead just getting a *"Well done."* Let's keep up their lust for life, and learning by joining them in being proud of their achievements.

CHAPTER 17

Meeting your own needs

I have written about the importance of identifying and meeting the needs of your child, but it's very difficult to meet the needs of others when we have unmet needs of our own. When you are feeling drained and out of patience, it is so important that you stop and think, identifying what it is that *you* are feeling and what it is that you need. And go further than that. Find a way to meet those needs.

The idea that we have to live in constant conflict, *"Your needs against mine,"* is unnecessary. Get creative and find a way that everyone can be a winner.

> Your children deserve a vibrant parent living a life of passion and fun. A thriving adult to look up to and be proud of.

Taking care of your own needs is not selfish. We all need to get enough sleep, to have time to eat, think, dream, create and just be. We need conversation and socialisation. Your own needs are in essence very similar to those of your child's. It makes sense then that when you try to meet their needs without addressing your own, you will struggle.

In the same way that your toddler displays her unmet needs with crying, hitting out or seemingly irrational behaviours, your unmet needs will show themselves in a lack of patience, creativity and spontaneity. Perhaps you will shout more, or say no unnecessarily. Perhaps you will take it out on your partner, or beat yourself up about all the things you think you are doing wrong. If you have made it this far along in this book, I know you want to give your children the very best in life. You want to be the best parent you can be. Start at the roots and give yourself the tools you need to make it happen.

Life with a toddler can be so busy you never seem to find the time to meet your own needs, so it is vital that you put yourself up near the top of your list of priorities, just as you do with your child. If you are desperate for sleep, make sure you do everything you can to meet that need. Rest if he takes a nap, prioritising your sleep over housework or keeping busy. Go to bed when your child does for a few days to maximise the hours you have in bed. Even if you are woken frequently, just laying in bed is more restful than watching TV or staying up to get on with things.

Seek support everywhere you can. Our natural state is to live in tribes sharing childcare between the whole extended family. We live in a time of huge isolation, in tiny families, often as single parents. This puts a lot of pressure and strain on the nuclear family.

It is vital to find support where you can, and accept offers of help. If no offers come your way, don't be afraid to ask. This doesn't have to be in the form of childcare if you prefer not to leave your child. It can be in the form of company, shared cooking, running errands or just the offer of a listening ear.

It can be so easy to feel like you are the only one in the world doing things a bit differently, especially when every other mother you encounter is conforming to mainstream parenting styles, and telling you where you are going wrong. But there are others out there feeling just the same as you. There are groups for everything from breastfeeding and baby wearing, to home educating and attachment parenting. Groups where people are not closed off to different ideas, where you don't have to tick all the boxes to fit in and make friends.

The internet is a wonderful resource, utilise it to find your own tribe.

CHAPTER 18

Trust your child, trust yourself

Throughout this book my message has hopefully been one of trust. Society tells us to ignore our instincts, to listen to the experts, to train our children and override their own needs and feelings with those of our own. This is not a view I agree with.

Our children ARE trustworthy. Your instincts are not a sign of weakness. Throughout the ages our instincts have proved to be right, ensuring the survival of the species by protecting our children, loving them unconditionally and listening to our hearts. Discipline is such a huge issue in current parenting trends, and it need not be. So many of the behavioural issues that come up are down to poor role modelling, too much control and restricted love.

> You absolutely cannot spoil a child with love and hugs.

Our children are pushed too soon to be independent. This however, will always backfire, creating children who cling, who regress, who act without caution or respect for others.

Children who are secure in their relationships to their primary care givers, who are accepted fully, treated fairly and shown the way by a strong, loving and secure role model, will find independence without any additional assistance, in their own time.

Children are capable of so much more than we give them credit for. Given the right circumstances and parenting, children are able to make sensible choices, understand and respect their boundaries, and treat others with the same love and respect they are used to receiving. Of course, children are not hemmed into the same boxes as us adults. Their choices may be far more creative than those we might have made for them, and this is how, if we let ourselves and our preconceptions go, we can learn so much from our children.

Educating and informing ourselves on options that meet the whole families needs, which parent in partnership, and avoid conflict, gives us the power to return to instinctive, responsive and authentic parenting. Seeing the difference that these changes make in our relationships with our children, will provide us with the confidence to ignore the expectations of others, the "shoulds" and the "can'ts". Instead, we can focus on making the best decisions to meet the needs of our own families.

Parenting is an incredible and rewarding journey, and the early years are over so quickly. While other parents may wish the terrible twos away, I hope this book has provided you with the tools to stay in the moment, savouring the sheer brilliance that is your child. You are an incredible parent and no one will ever be able to convince you otherwise when you have given over your trust to your child. The bond and partnership you have will be all it takes to convince you.

Love yourself, Love life, Love your children, Love Parenting.

Resources

The Inuit Way, A guide to Inuit culture produced by Pauktuutit Inuit Women of Canada

Child Raising In Non-violent Cultures, Creating a culture that chooses non-violence with intention. By Sarah McElroy

About the author

 Samantha Vickery is the creator of www.loveparenting.org. She is wildly passionate about parenting as nature intended, and is striving to raise her son with trust for his biological instincts and respect for his independence. She created Love Parenting to provide information and inspiration to parents who want to bring more natural, gentle and mindful practices into their parenting, and aid them in finding the joy in trusting their instincts and most importantly, their children.

Sam has worked with children from birth to teens, with and without additional needs and in a wide range of settings. She has dedicated her time to learning how to get results, forging stress free relationships and seeing happier children in the process. She has found time and time again, that once a connection is formed, less behavioural issues and more cooperation are the result.

In her spare time (if she isn't writing) she can be found reading. Devouring books of all kinds from parenting literature to novels. Her days are spent searching for snails, jumping on beds, reading in dens and walking through the forest, with the best little companion in the whole world.

Sam believes that parenting can be an incredible and joyful experience, and shares her advice on making this a reality within her writing. Her goal is to enable children and parents everywhere to have the lives they deserve, filled with love, nature, connection and respect.

47749182R00108

Made in the USA
Lexington, KY
12 December 2015